Lifetales

Workbook

Writing Your Life Stories

Karen Hamilton Silvestri

Karenzo Media
St. Pauls, NC

Lifetales Workbook Writing Your Life Stories

by Karen Hamilton Silvestri

2007, 2009
2nd edition 2014

Layout: Karen Hamilton Silvestri
Cover Design: Karen Hamilton Silvestri
All clip art by Mark A. Hicks, illustrator for Discovery School's Clip Art Gallery.

Karenzo Media
www.karenzomedia.net

Writing exercise handouts may be photocopied for personal use and/or educational use.

ISBN 978-0-9899318-8-5

Printed in the USA

Dedicated
to all those
whose stories
are now lost.

For help with writing your Lifetales or if you would like to join a class, email
Karen at karenzomedia@gmail.com

Please leave a review of this book wherever you purchased it! I'll be happy to review YOUR book when it comes it!

TABLE OF CONTENTS

Introduction

I originally started this workbook back in 1999. It didn't go into a first printing until 2007. It still is only sold in print in very few places. Digital sales are higher, as they tend to be. But my plan for the workbook was that it would be something that even people with no writing experience could sit down with and WRITE IN. Digital just doesn't work that way.

So, it is time – past time – to update the workbook and make it available to you in print form, so that you can start writing your lifetales! Since I wrote the introduction (see below), lifewriting has virtually exploded around the world. Everyone, it seems, is writing their memoirs. Check out Amazon or any major retailer, and you will see thousands of self-published (and traditionally published) memoirs.

Isn't it time for YOU to join the collective story? Isn't it time for you to start preserving YOUR part in history?

Let's get started!

Original Introduction

With the publication of *Angela's Ashes* by Frank McCourt, the art of Lifewriting has become a huge topic of interest to the American public. The July 2002 issue of Writer's Digest is almost wholly devoted to Lifewriting and the publishers of Writer's Digest have even issued a separate magazine to cover the how-to's of writing memoirs and journaling.

In 1999 I began teaching memoir and journaling classes in Palm Beach County. I have taught workshops at Borders Bookstore in Boynton Beach, Prosperity Oaks in Palm Beach Gardens, and to individual groups. I also work as a Personal Historian, taping clients' memoirs and transcribing them to book form.

A few of the topics I explore with readers are:

- ❖ Why should we write our memoirs?
- ❖ Basic Writing Rules for Memoirs
- ❖ Dealing with Painful Issues, Truth, and Personal Myths
- ❖ Items to include in your memoir
- ❖ Interviewing Friends and Family Members
- ❖ Research
- ❖ Putting it all Together
- ❖ Re-writes
- ❖ Publishing Your Memoirs
- ❖ Getting professional assistance

Some Definitions of Memoir, Autobiography, and Biography

Memoir	Autobiography	Biography
Factually accurate timeline of someone's emotional journey*	Factually accurate timeline of someone's life*	Factually accurate (backed up with research) of a third party*
A *slice* of an autobiography	A person's life story - their entire life span to date	Written history of a person's life
A snapshot of a period in a person's life that provided a turning point		

* When it comes to autobiography and memoir because memory is subjective *even to itself*. What one views as fact at age 20 is largely different from what one views as fact at age 50.

Characteristics of the Memoir Form

Memoir	Autobiography
Focus on a brief period of time or series of related events	Covers a person's entire life to date
Many of the usual elements of storytelling	Does not usually use elements of storytelling
A fictional quality even though the story is true	True account of a person's life
Therapeutic experience for the memoirist	Therapeutic experience for the writer
Includes the author's feelings and thoughts	Includes the author's feelings and thoughts

About Lifewriting

We all think that we are not famous enough to write our memoirs but this is a misconception! What would you do if you came upon a manuscript written by your great grandmother in the late 1800's?? Wouldn't you be thrilled beyond words to hear what life was like then? Wouldn't you be excited to find that people then loved, lost, and lived much as you do today?? How did they handle it? How did everyday life make them feel??

Why should we write our memoirs?

- To remember and honor our lives.
- To bring our family members together.
- To bring new insight to our lives.
- To provide future generations a look at life as we knew it.
- To facilitate a healing experience within our lives.
- To connect us to history.

"People today are rootless and aching for connections to the past", says Lettice Stuart, a Texas personal historian who records the memoirs of everyday people. The process of documenting their lives often brings family members together and, as their life tale unfolds they will find themselves gaining new insights into events that took place, perhaps even bringing about healing to the past.

It is the *act of writing,* not the words themselves that produce a healing in the writer. Therefore, one need not be a scholar or novelist to reap the benefits of lifewriting.

What is Memoir Therapy?

An excerpt from "Putting Back Together the Broken World with Words" by Karen Y. Hamilton

Memoir Therapy is a form of autobiographical writing. It asks several questions:

- o Where is our true story?
- o Where is our true myth?
- o Is there truth in our story at all?

There are many versions of a life - all are true, all are fiction - it depends on the time in which the life is being told. Sociologist Robert Elbaz states, "Autobiography is fiction, and fiction is autobiography. Factual truth is irrelevant to autobiography." We change our story in order to create ourselves but is it our self we are creating or the self as a cog in the wheel of society? The memoir writer has the opportunity to re-create the world they live in as well as themselves.

In Memoir Therapy, the goal is to uncover the many selves that we have lived. By so doing, we are able to ferret out those selves that we have allowed societal influences to create for us and move into a more authentic self. The words we bring to the page create a myth of our personal self.

By definition a myth is something that *was* true but now is probably not. By recording our memoirs, our myths, we provide ourselves the healing power of words to transform our story. And the more we write the more healing we bring to ourselves. It is through the serial memoir that memoir approaches its true and ultimate form, an account through time of a person's life, a story with many beginnings that does not end until the author himself reaches the end. And even then, the story continues, doesn't it?

We gather strength from our words, from our stories. We set into motion a flood of communication that brings us healing. We listen to, we read, we write words, words, words - *the meaning of the word is superfluous, it changes every time we reach for a new creation of our self.* And isn't that all that matters in the end, that the stories themselves, not their meaning, give us the power to create ourselves?

Introduction to Workshop

Why do you want to write your life stories?

_____

_____

_____

_____

_____

_____

_____

_____

_____

_____

_____

_____

_____

_____

_____

_____

_____

_____

_____

_____

_____

_____

_____

_____

_____

What do you hope to get out of this workshop?

_____

_____

_____

_____

_____

_____

_____

_____

_____

_____

_____

_____

_____

_____

_____

_____

_____

_____

_____

_____

_____

_____

Peer Editing in a Workshop

o Listen quietly while the author reads their piece. Don't interrupt them.

o Make notes on your Peer Response sheet.

o Never attack the author.

o Never criticize the author.

o Always say at least one thing that you liked about the piece.

Peer Response Worksheet

❖ **Three aspects of the piece that I liked**

1._____

_____

2._____

_____

3._____

_____

❖ **Three puzzling or confusing aspects of the piece to me**

1._____

_____

2._____

_____

3._____

_____

❖ **Three suggestions for improvement that I have for the piece**

1._____

_____

2._____

_____

3._____

_____

Your Inner Critic

The inner critic is that voice in your head that keeps telling you that you can't do this. "You're not a writer," it keeps saying to you every time you sit down to write something.

Block your inner critic by embracing it. Let it have its say then gently tell it that now it is your turn.

1. Write a letter to your inner critic. Talk to it and give it voice. Leave nothing out. When your inner critic feels the need to jump in while you are writing, let it state its mind quickly, then gently remind it that it is your turn now.

_____

_____

_____

_____

_____

_____

_____

_____

_____

_____

_____

_____

_____

_____

_____

_____

_____

_____

_____

_____

_____

2. What does your Inner Critic say to you? Have a dialogue with your Critic in the chart below.

Your Critic	You
Ex: You are a lousy writer.	*Maybe, but at least I am writing!*

Rules for Writing

These are not really rules! They are more like gentle reminders!

- ✓ Start with one story at a time.

- ✓ Make a schedule to write at least one page every day and stick to it!

- ✓ Remember to include your feelings about the event! Many men forget to do this!

- ✓ If you write only one page per day, you will have 365 pages in one year!

- ✓ Use vivid detail.

- ✓ For now, ignore spelling and grammar. If you worry about getting every sentence perfect, you will never finish your writing!

- ✓ You can check facts later. Don't worry if you forgot someone's name or a particular date-just get the story written!!! You can go back later!

- ✓ You may want to alter names and identities to protect your loved ones.

Getting Started

The Timeline

The important thing to keep in mind is that you will never get your memoir written unless you start! Start anywhere but START!

I find it easiest when teaching writing classes to begin with lists, progress to sentences then paragraphs, and finally put it all together. I suggest that you do the same. Make list after list after list – this way you will never have a reason to cry Writer's Block because your list of writing ideas is right on hand.

We will begin with the…**TIMELINE**

The backbone of your lifestories is your Timeline. This is an extended chart of the relationships and events that have shaped your life. These are the people and events that have made you the person you are today.

EVENTS IN YOUR LIFE: Here are a few to get you started: • an illness or a death in the family • the arrival of a sibling • the ethnic group you grew up in • the religious group you grew up in • a certain relationship with a peer • a failure or success at school • a decision you made to do or not do something • an external event such as a fire, flood, tornado, auto accident • marriage • children • career choices • spiritual experiences • divorce

This is but a few of the major events that turn a person's life to one direction or the other. The list you make may be many pages long or relatively short. This depends on the individual. You may add to this list as you remember things. Include everything you can think of that had any impact on your life.

ASSIGNMENT: Make a timeline of your life.

childhood...teen years...young adult...middle age...senior years

or

birth..1-12..13-18..19-30..30-50..50-70..70-100

Mark pivotal points on the timeline as reference points in your writing.

Find your BEFORE/AFTER moment. What is the point – that dividing line – when something so pivotal happened that it changed you forever? You may have more than one of them.
After completing your timeline, do the exercises on the following pages.

Sample Timeline Worksheet

(excerpted from The Brooklyn Hobo by Alex Procho)

Birth	1-12	13-18	19-30	30-50
Born in upstate NY 1951 2 siblings, triplets Single mother	Mother hospitalized Moved to Brooklyn, age 10 Father, Mafia connections	Don't fit in, all teen years Woodstock Vietnam Left home to travel across country Drugs and hippies Rehab	Hitched a ride on a freight train Attended several Colleges Met crazy people while hitchhiking across country Daughter born Rehab	Married several Times Another daughter Born Rehab again Father dies 50th birthday and the Twin Towers

* Filling out the timeline of events will help you to pinpoint those events in your life that had the most impact, the events that made you the person you are today. When you are finished filling out all the events that you can remember, circle the most important ones. That is where you will find your stories.

Blank Timeline Worksheet

Assignment:
Write ten relationships and/or events that were the most crucial in shaping your life.

The foundation of your lifestories is your Relationship & Event Lists. These are extended lists of the relationships and events that have shaped your life. These are the people and events that have made you the person you are today. Who are the people who played a major role in your life? What are some of the events that had an impact on your life?

Make a list of relationships and events that impacted your life. Refer to your timeline if you want.

RELATIONSHIPS	EVENTS

Crucial Relationships & Events

Make a list of the crucial events in your life. Start with your birth (did something extraordinary happen when you were born?) and then move on through your childhood, young adult years, middle age, etc. from those events, can you choose one that impacted your life the most?

Relationships

1._____

2._____

3._____

4._____

5._____

6._____

7._____

8._____

9._____

10._____

Events

1._____

2._____

3._____

4._____

5._____

6._____

7._____

8._____

9._____

10._____

Central Theme

There is within your life a **central theme – life change**. Choose one of the events from your Lists. When you have isolated an event, look at it from all angles and write down its key points. **Use the cluster map to help you map it out. Each one of the clusters can become a paragraph in your story!**

How old were you? What was happening in the world at that time? What was the value or moral code that existed at that time and how did it affect the event? How did all of these factors come together to create your epiphany?

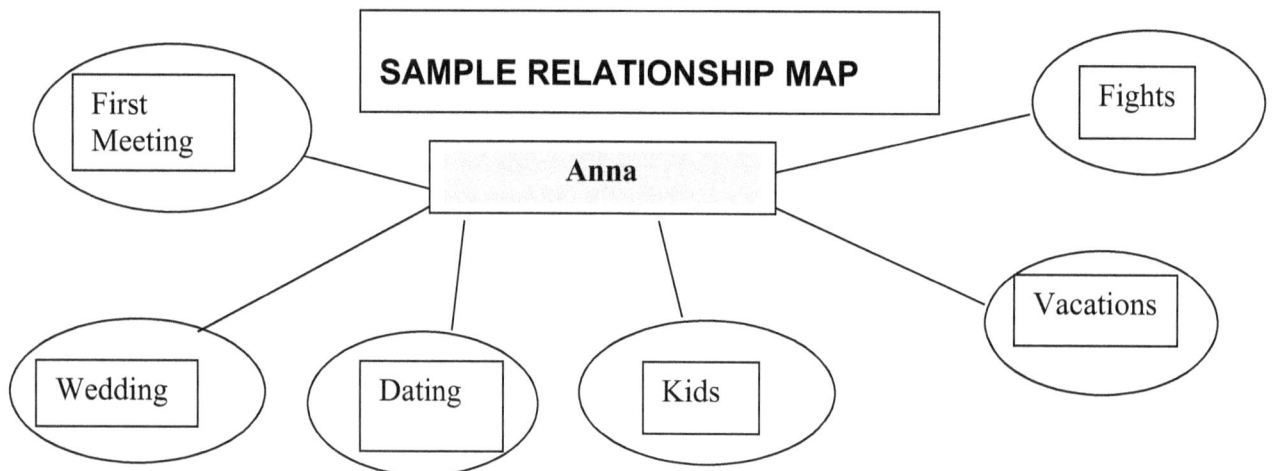

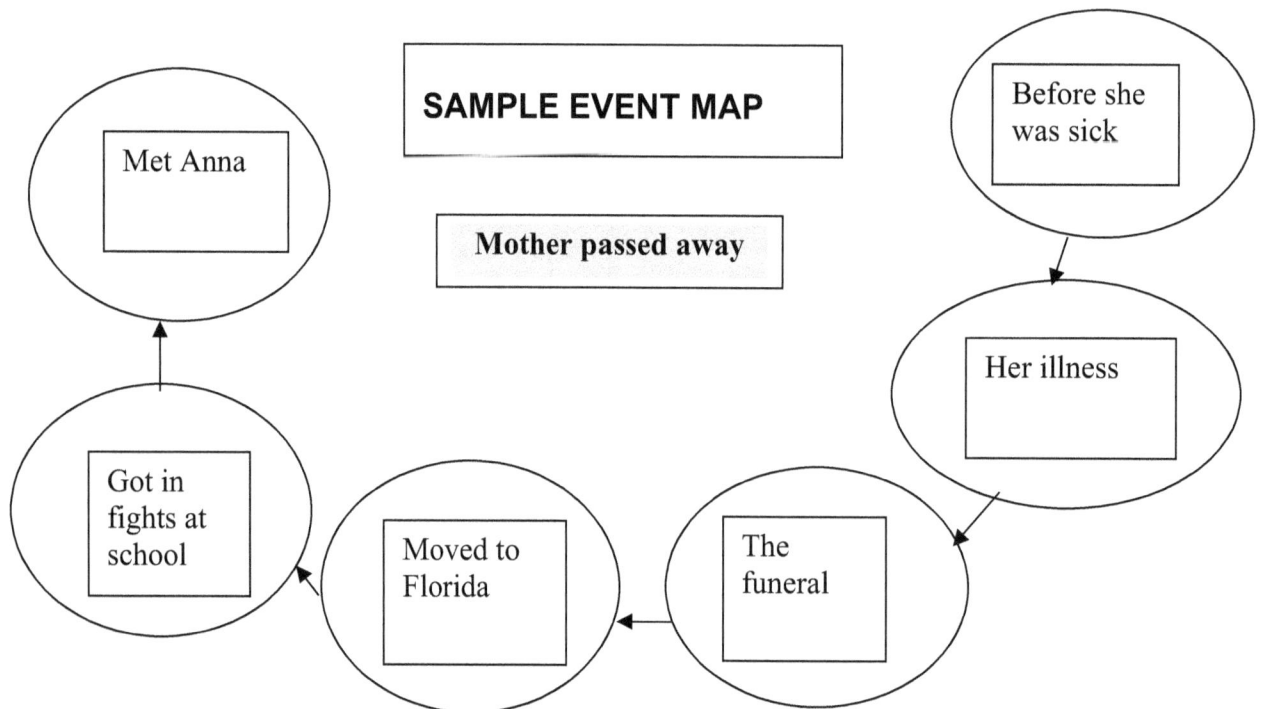

SAMPLE RELATIONSHIP MAP

- Anna
  - First Meeting
  - Fights
  - Vacations
  - Wedding
  - Dating
  - Kids

SAMPLE EVENT MAP

Mother passed away

- Met Anna
- Before she was sick
- Her illness
- The funeral
- Moved to Florida
- Got in fights at school

BLANK RELATIONSHIP MAP

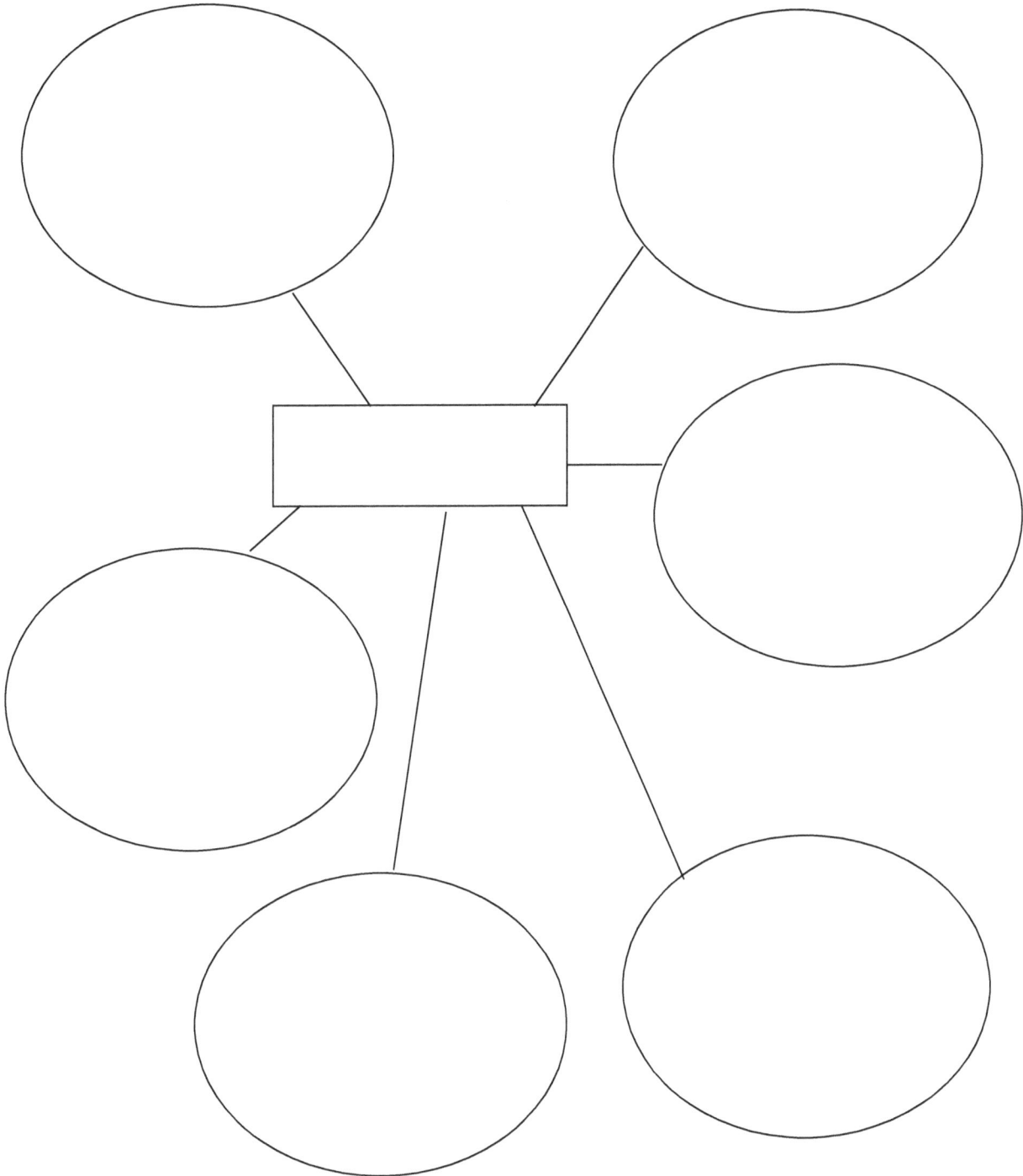

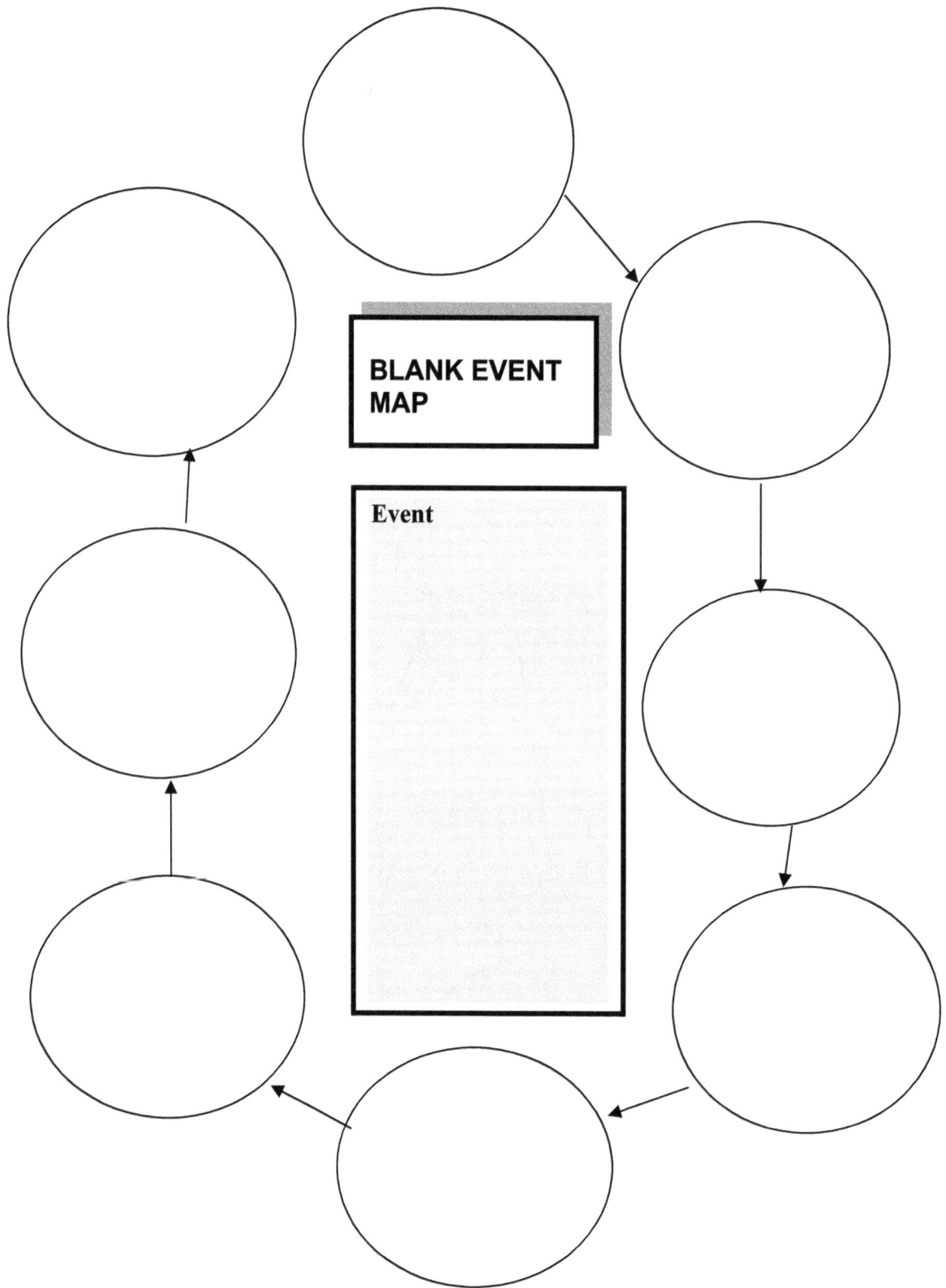

BLANK EVENT MAP

Event

Now that you have the key details mapped out, tell us about one of the events. **Don't think about publishing it**. Just pretend your children or grandchildren are gathered at your feet and you are going to tell them a story.

Once upon a time I…

_____

_____

_____

_____

_____

_____

_____

_____

_____

_____

_____

_____

_____

_____

_____

_____

_____

_____

_____

_____

_____

_____

_____

_____

_____

The Five Senses

To make your writing come alive on the page, remember to always ask yourself:

_ What do I see?

_ What do I hear?

_ What do I smell?

_ What can I touch and how does it feel?

_ What am I feeling right now?

Apply the five senses questions to every scene you write!

You will be amazed how much you left out!

FAVORITES

Writing about a favorite thing, person, or place gives you short vignettes that you can add to your larger memoir. Perhaps the paragraph about your favorite house will fit in with your overall theme of moving and loss.

Practice writing about each favorite – even if it seems silly – the act of remembering and writing will keep your creative energy flowing. Try to write at least a full paragraph about each thing. **Remember! Use your five senses!**

Here are just a few favorites – I'm sure you can think of some of your own!

A Sample Favorites Paragraph

This short paragraph was from a memory of my mother-in-law's favorite pastime with her father when she was growing up on Coney Island. It is written in the third person.

> *Isadore taking Leah to see the trains.*
>
> The train smelled like hard-boiled eggs. She sat on the empty luggage cart swinging her legs and rubbing her little hands together in anticipation. If she strained her ears she could just make out the far off chooo-chooo as the train rumbled its way into town. Her father stood behind Leah, straight and tall and adjusted his starched collar.

- ❑ Book as a child
- ❑ Book as an adult
- ❑ Meal
- ❑ Food
- ❑ Song/music
- ❑ Pet
- ❑ Toy as a child
- ❑ Place in the world
- ❑ House you lived in
- ❑ Gift you received
- ❑ TV show
- ❑ Movie
- ❑ Dance
- ❑ Teacher
- ❑ Flower
- ❑ Holiday
- ❑ Poem
- ❑ Novel
- ❑ Scripture

My Favorites Paragraphs

_____
_____
_____
_____
_____
_____
_____
_____
_____
_____
_____
_____
_____
_____
_____
_____
_____
_____
_____
_____
_____
_____
_____
_____
_____

FIRSTS

Firsts Introduction

As with Favorites, Firsts lead you into deeper territory. The first anything is usually a memorable experience and quite often marks a change in our lives.

Again, try to write at least a paragraph for each suggested topic. Remember, these paragraphs can be fitted into your larger memoir.

Remember! Use your five senses!

❏ Kiss

❏ Girlfriend/boyfriend

❏ Date

❏ Car

❏ Pet

❏ Job

❏ Bike

❏ Trip alone

❏ Child born

❏ Broken bone

❏ Hospital stay

❏ Broken heart

❏ Loss of a loved one

❏ Marriage proposal

❏ Teacher you can remember

❏ Bank account

❏ Time you learned to swim

❏ Ride a bike

Add your own first

A sample First paragraph

The First House I Remember Living In

We lived on Florida Mango Street, a typical street of suburban houses that all looked the same. Don't ask me the year we moved there – midsixties somewhere - a place of backyard barbecues, cookie baking housewives, and mammoth cars of various pastel colors. Everything was pastel – the houses, the cars, and the women. My world was a swirl of muted pinks, blues, greens, and yellows. We had two concrete swans that stood sentinel watch at the front door. The driveway was a half moon. The back yard stretched for an eternity in my child's eye, muted green grasses waving invitingly and daring my father to take out the mower and slice paths through the tangles. Which he did from time to time, sometimes waiting for the grass to reach a height of almost out-of-control - a metaphor for our lives, for life in general – out-of-control.

Daddy would plod along in long strides pushing the mower through the overgrown field of grass while we trooped along behind him in the paths he made. The towers of grass on either side of us formed the walls of a maze and it was our job to follow our leader while he led us to safety. I was always depressed when the job was finished and the jungle became just another postage stamp yard like everyone else's. Common. I never wanted to be common.

My Firsts Paragraphs

MAPS

Draw a map to the house of your childhood.

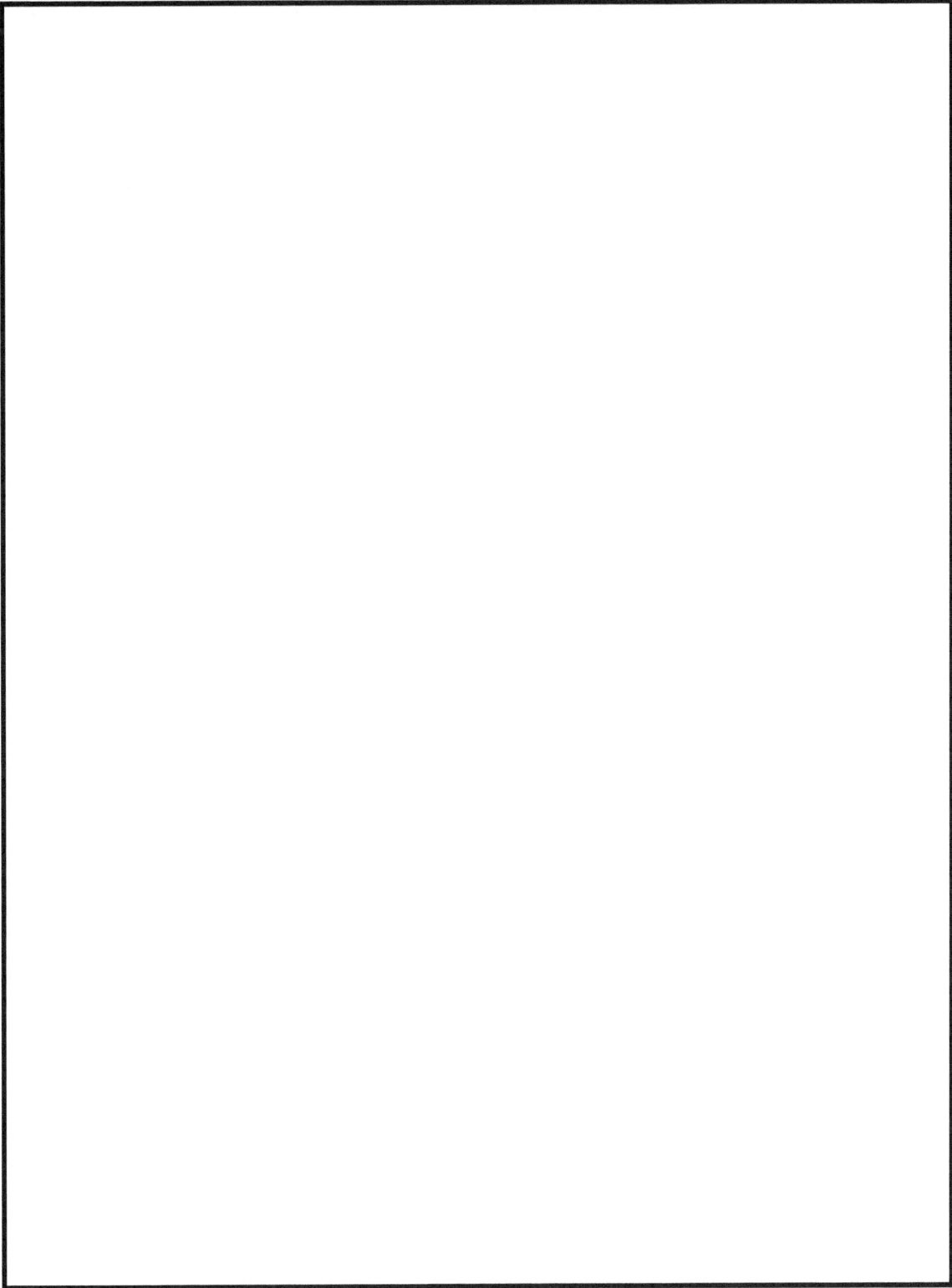

Sketch out a diagram of the house. Now tell what your room looked like. Where did the family spend most of their time? Did you have a secret hide-away?

Now, write about the house that you drew. Using your five senses, tell us about the house and the occupants.

_____

_____

_____

_____

_____

_____

_____

_____

_____

_____

_____

_____

_____

_____

_____

_____

_____

_____

_____

_____

_____

_____

_____

Truth in Memoir

Masks

Everyday, we switch masks to fit the occasion we find ourselves in. When we are talking with our child's teacher we assume the 'parent' mask. When we talk to our doctor, some of us assume the 'victim' mask.

I am very good at masks! If you spend one day being conscious of your different personas, you will be astonished at how many 'masks' you wear in one day!

Make it a point to watch out for your masks!

Not all masks are harmful, but they are still masks! And the definition of mask is to cover up something. In this case, you are covering up YOUR STORIES!

"An autobiography may be largely fictional. Few can recall clear details of their early life and are therefore dependent on other people's impressions, of necessity equally unreliable. Moreover, everyone tends to remember what he wants to remember. Disagreeable facts are sometimes glossed over or repressed ...." Cuddon, J. A. The Penguin Dictionary of Literary Terms and Literary

Assignment:
List a few of the masks that you wear. What does your work mask like? Your family mask? Church mask? Etc....

> Assignment:
> Write about your saddest life experience.

_____

_____

_____

_____

_____

_____

_____

_____

_____

_____

_____

_____

_____

_____

_____

_____

_____

_____

_____

_____

_____

_____

_____

_____

_____

Truth

"Writing must take on difficult subjects and seek to fairly express hard, buried, denied, painful truths, but in so doing it contributes to our mutual benefit, to a wider social, human good." The Portable MFA in Creative Writing"

Assignment: What is the one thing you are afraid to have people know about you?

_____

_____

_____

_____

_____

_____

_____

_____

_____

_____

_____

_____

_____

_____

_____

_____

_____

_____

_____

_____

_____

_____

_____

_____

Assignment: What masks do you wear? What 'myths' surrounded you as you grew up?

_____

_____

_____

_____

_____

_____

_____

_____

_____

_____

_____

_____

_____

_____

_____

_____

_____

_____

_____

_____

_____

_____

_____

_____

_____

Sample Truths Writing

Parakeets
From *Tales of the Brooklyn Hobo* by Alex Procho

Mom, who was on amphetamines, bought two parakeets. The cage hung in the living room. Parakeets are extremely noisy, especially in the morning at sunrise. I sometimes wonder if my mom acquired them on purpose, to annoy my dad and prove her individuality, or maybe a way to do anything to get his attention.

As I was watching my cartoons that morning – Bugs Bunny, The Howdie Doody Show, The Mickey Mouse Club – I hear my dad at the top of his voice yelling, "Shut those fucking birds up!" Mommy walks by, enjoying his misery, sort of like getting back at him for his night life and running around with friends and lovers and neglecting her and his kids. A door slams open. I anticipate the known.

Six foot two and 210 pounds of rage enter the room. He grabs this birdcage of birds, being held prisoner against their own will as I see it, and he opens the front door and hurls the cage of birds onto the street. Mommy screams, "What are you doing?" He looks at her with satisfaction, "You and your birds should only die," he says in a smug way.

Beth and Carey awaken, not knowing what just took place. They will not remember this incident later in life. I take all this in and will relive it in my mind over and over again for the rest of my life. Mommy is crying. "You son of a bitch." And the birds lay dead on Tuttle Avenue. I can't watch my mother retrieving the dead birds and burying them. No one mentions anything – it is all swept under the rug of insanity once again.

Truths Worksheet

_____

_____

_____

_____

_____

_____

_____

_____

_____

_____

_____

_____

_____

_____

_____

_____

_____

_____

_____

_____

_____

_____

_____

Items to include in your memoir

- ✓ Photographs, maps, and/or drawings of places you lived

- ✓ Photographs, maps, and/or drawings of places you visited

- ✓ Photographs, maps, and/or drawings of places you went to school

- ✓ Photographs, maps, and/or drawings of places you worked

- ✓ The history of the town you grew up in

- ✓ Newspaper clippings of events that happened in your lifetime

- ✓ Favorite poems or essays

- ✓ Favorite songs

- ✓ Your own creative endeavors (photographs, poetry, stories, drawings, etc.)

Assignment:
Write a short vignette related to one of the items above.
Why did you choose it? What does it mean to you?

_____

_____

_____

_____

_____

_____

_____

_____

_____

_____

_____

_____

_____

_____

_____

_____

_____

_____

_____

_____

_____

_____

_____

PHOTOS

Assignment:
Look through old photos and write about the stories behind them. Let the photo transport you back in time.

_____
_____
_____
_____
_____
_____
_____
_____
_____
_____
_____
_____
_____
_____
_____
_____
_____
_____
_____
_____
_____
_____
_____
_____

IMAGINE

Pretend you are catching up old classmates on your life. Imagine you get together with old friends or family.

What are some of the stories you would share? Make a list of all the stories you would tell your old friends.

_____

_____

_____

_____

_____

_____

_____

_____

_____

_____

_____

_____

_____

_____

_____

_____

_____

_____

_____

_____

_____

_____

Now tell one of those stories here!

_____

_____

_____

_____

_____

_____

_____

_____

_____

_____

_____

_____

_____

_____

_____

_____

_____

_____

_____

_____

_____

_____

_____

_____

_____

_____

_____

Constructing the Memoir

Elements of a Story

> **William Zinsser says, *"Good memoirs are a careful act of construction"***

What are the elements of "construction" that the storyteller or memoir writer controls?

❖ Characterization

❖ Voice

❖ Event

❖ Setting

❖ Plot development

Characterization

Think about the people in your life. These are the characters that will people your stories. Make a list of all the key characters in your life. Sometimes it helps to complete a character on each person that you can refer back to from time to time.

You can make your characters come alive by remembering to *show* who they are and what *your feelings* are towards them. Don't just tell your readers about them – make them come alive by having them move, talk, *act*. Remember the writer's rule – **SHOW, DON'T TELL**.

> # Assignment:
> ## List some of the characters in your story.

_____

_____

_____

_____

_____

_____

_____

_____

_____

_____

_____

_____

_____

_____

_____

Voice

Every person has his or her own voice. You can tell much about a person by the way they talk – where they may be from, what their current attitude is, and whether they are introverted or extroverted. The same is true about a writer's voice. Barbara Taylor Bradford writes in a much different voice than Franz Kafka. We know authors by their voice.

As you begin writing, you will probably have no idea what your voice is and that is okay. As with a choice of clothes, you may choose a different voice for different writings. For the Memoir, the voice you use should be as close to your personality as possible. In other words, the voice should be true and honest. Forget publishing, forget other people reading your words, and just write as if you were telling a story to a friend or writing in your journal.

> ## Assignment:
> If a movie were made of your life, what star would play you? Why?

_____

_____

_____

_____

_____

_____

_____

_____

_____

_____

_____

_____

_____

_____

_____

Point of View

<table>
<tr><td>

First-Person Point of View

This is the POV that most writers of Memoir and Autobiography use. The main character is the author of the story (not necessarily YOU!).

</td><td>

Third-Person Point of View

This is the commonly used form of POV. The story is told through multiple characters.

</td></tr>
</table>

Assignment:

Write about how you met your spouse (or how your parents met) in the third person. (Samples of this assignment are on the next few pages.)

_____

_____

_____

_____

_____

_____

_____

_____

_____

_____

Sample First Person Essay

How They Met

The Bolita man just left. The man always talks too much. Here I sit with all this washing to get done and that man has to come a-knocking on my door. I don't believe in gambling and I tell him that every time he shows up here – which is once a week, right after payday at the Naval Yard because he knows folks has got the money then for such foolishness. He's sweet on little Jo – that's how come he talks so blame much. Damn Bolita man. I tell him every week that Jo is only twelve years old and she sure as hell wouldn't take up with a scraggly little Cuban man selling lottery tickets.

That's a lie, actually. The only reason I know Jo wouldn't take up with the likes of him is because I know she is smitten with my boy, Ernest. Not that I approve of that match either, mind you. Ernest just turned twenty and has been off these six months in London, England. He looks so smart in his Air Force uniform. I guess I can understand why Jo is so taken with him.

My boy came home yesterday. He came a-strutting down the back alley of our house on Watson Street looking like his Daddy used to look when he would come home from hunting, all puffed up with pride and knowing how good he looked. I still ache inside remembering the loss of that man. And I ache even more with the loss to Ernest of knowing his Daddy – Bill never even knew Ernest was coming when he died out there in them swamps.

Anyway, they don't know I was watching when Ernest turned that corner into the alley looking so fine. Jo was lending me a hand with the young-un's and had taken them out for a stroll in the carriage. She is such an itty-bitty thing but developing too damn fast in my opinion. Men's eyes take to rolling back in their damn heads whenever Josephine Garcia goes strolling by. Ernest hadn't seen that little girl for several years – he being off to the war and her still at least looking like a child when he left. So I watched from the window as he rounded the corner in his smart Air Force uniform, head cocked to one side and duffel bag thrown over his left shoulder. And I watched as Jo looked up from fussing with baby Tommy's diaper and caught sight of my boy coming down that alley.

I expect I knew then there was nothing I could do about it. But it worries me fearsome, I can tell you that. That little scrap of a child-woman doesn't have a chance. And neither does my boy. I saw the whole thing though they don't know it. And I done lived long enough on this world to know those two fool children done fell in love with each other and they don't even know it yet.

Well, I best get back to my washing.

Sample Third Person Essay

How They Met

Flo sank down into tattered sofa. The Bolita Man had just left. The man always talked too much. She had so much washing to get done and that man had to come a-knocking on her door. Flo didn't believe in gambling and she told him that every time he showed up – which was once a week, right after payday at the Naval Yard because he knows folks has got the money then for such foolishness. The Bolita Man was sweet on little Jo – that's how come he talked so blame much. Damn Bolita man, she thought. She told him every week that Jo was only twelve years old and she sure as hell wouldn't take up with a scraggly little Cuban man selling lottery tickets.

But Flo knew that was a lie. The only reason she knew Jo wouldn't take up with the likes of the Bolita Man was because she knew Jo was smitten with her boy, Ernest. Not that she approved of that match either, mind you. Ernest just turned twenty and had been off these six months in London, England. Flo smiled to herself as she pictured Ernest in his Air Force uniform. "I reckon I can understand why Jo is so taken with him." she said to herself.

Ernest had come home yesterday. He came a-strutting down the back alley of their little house on Watson Street looking like his Daddy used to look when he would come home from hunting, all puffed up with pride and knowing how good he looked. Flo still ached inside remembering the loss of that man. And she ached even more with the loss to Ernest of knowing his Daddy – Bill never even knew Ernest was coming when he died out there in them swamps.

Anyway, Ernest and Josephine didn't know Flo was watching when Ernest turned that corner into the alley looking so fine. Jo was lending her a hand with the young-un's and had taken them out for a stroll in the carriage. Just last week Flo had told her daughter-in-law, Connie, "That Josephine is such an itty-bitty pretty thing but developing too damn fast in my opinion." And it was true. Men's eyes took to rolling back in their damn heads whenever Josephine Garcia went strolling by. Ernest hadn't seen that little girl for several years – he being off to the war and her still at least looking like a child when he left. So Flo stood on the back porch and watched from the window as he rounded the corner in his smart Air Force uniform, head cocked to one side and duffel bag thrown over his left shoulder. And she watched as Jo looked up from fussing with baby Tommy's diaper and caught sight of that handsome soldier boy coming down that alley. Hell, the sight took even Flo's breath away.

Flo figured there was nothing she could do about it. But it worried her fearsome. That little scrap of a child-woman didn't have a chance. And neither did Ernest. Flo saw the whole thing though they didn't know she knew. And she figured she had done lived long enough on this world to know those two fool children done fell in love with each other and they don't even know it yet.

Event = Emotional experience

Sample Emotional events:

❖ A nightmare

❖ A birth

❖ Visit to doctor/dentist

❖ A time you got hurt emotionally

❖ A time you got hurt physically

❖ A death

❖ A promise made

❖ A promise broken

❖ A neighborhood bully

❖ A time you were jealous

❖ A time you got very angry

❖ A trip you took

❖ An argument you had

Assignment: Write about an emotional event.

Setting

Use your five senses – sight, sound, taste, touch, smell – to help visualize your setting.

Consider how you want your reader to see the scene.

What will they see first?

What is the most important thing in the scene that you want them to see?

Consider the season, weather, time of day – incorporate these elements into your description.

Assignment: Write about your childhood home or write about your favorite place. Set the scene for your reader.

_____

_____

_____

_____

_____

Plot development

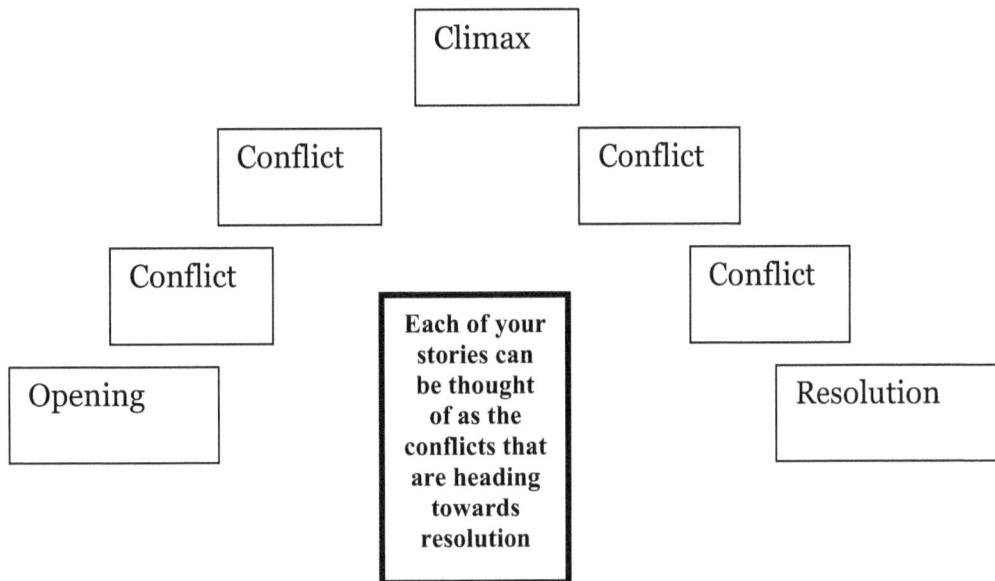

```
                        ┌──────────┐
                        │  Climax  │
                        └──────────┘
          ┌──────────┐          ┌──────────┐
          │ Conflict │          │ Conflict │
          └──────────┘          └──────────┘
     ┌──────────┐   ┌─────────────┐   ┌──────────┐
     │ Conflict │   │ Each of your │   │ Conflict │
     └──────────┘   │ stories can  │   └──────────┘
                    │ be thought   │
┌──────────┐        │ of as the    │      ┌──────────────┐
│ Opening  │        │ conflicts that│     │  Resolution  │
└──────────┘        │ are heading  │      └──────────────┘
                    │ towards      │
                    │ resolution   │
                    └─────────────┘
```

The definition of plot is the sequence of events. The sequence of events does not have to be linear. Many authors employ flashback – jumping back in time throughout the narrative to recall an earlier scene. The important thing to remember about plot is that the reader should be able to pick it out pretty quickly.

The plot generally contains some sort of conflict. This should be fairly easier for the Memoir writer since life is basically one conflict after another. Conflict is not necessarily something bad that happens. Conflict in the narrative sense occurs whenever something – good or bad – occurs that moves the characters further along towards some type of resolution.

If you follow the above chart, you will see that the sequence of events in a narrative always flows through conflict, even after the most important scene – the climax – occurs. The climax is the moment when everything comes to a head and the epiphany occurs. After that moment, the character has a few more conflicts to go through to reach the resolution. At the point of resolution, all the conflicts are resolved.

In all my studies of literature, I have determined that there really is no such thing as final resolution – especially in the Memoir or Autobiography. Stories always go on. The trend these days is to leave the story open – look at the series finale *The Soprano's*! Each of your stories can be thought of as the conflicts that are heading towards resolution – which will be the point you are currently at, sitting in front of this workbook writing.

Assignment: Make a list of your possible conflicts

_____
_____
_____
_____
_____
_____
_____
_____
_____
_____
_____
_____
_____
_____
_____
_____
_____
_____
_____
_____
_____
_____
_____
_____
_____
_____
_____
_____

Interviewing & Research

Interviewing

Successful Interviews

- o Prepare questions ahead of time. A good question leads to a *detailed* explanation.

- o Do background research about the person before the interview.

- o Ask open-ended questions, ones that require more than a yes or no answer.

- o Ask follow-up questions based on answers they might give.

- o Be prepared! Tape recorder, paper, pen, etc.

- o When taking notes, develop a shorthand that works for you – jot down key words instead of whole sentences – you can write it up later.

- o Try to not interrupt the person when they are talking. If you have a question or need clarification, jot a note on your pad and ask your question when they finish talking.

- o Always send a thank you note after the interview.

Assignment: Interview a member of your family. Jot down here possible questions you will ask.

Research

After conducting an interview on a family member, look at your notes and perform some detailed research on people and places that were mentioned.

> Did your relative stay in a hospital for a lengthy amount of time? Research the hospital.

> Where did the relative come from? Research the place – Odessa, Coney Island, Key West, Chicago, etc. You get the idea!

> Did your relative witness a world event? A battle? A natural disaster? Do some research on the event.

> ## Assignment: Research a member of your family. Jot down some notes here.

_____

_____

_____

_____

_____

_____

_____

_____

_____

_____

_____

_____

_____

_____

_____

_____

_____

_____

_____

_____

Layout and Printing

Lay Out a Book Manuscript in Microsoft Word

When you have written a novel, short story, or non-fiction book and are ready to have it printed, you need to know the basics of laying out the book on a word processor. Some self-publishing companies will do this job for you for a fee. However, you can do it yourself, if you know your way around MS Word. Depending on the version of MS Word that you have, navigating your way around may be a bit different but the tools are basically the same.

Choose the size that you want your book. Typical sizes for a book are 8.5 x 11, 6 x 9, and 5 x 8. These are the standard size for most self-published books. The larger size of the two is used for picture books, textbooks, and workbooks such as this one.

Use the "Page Setup" feature to set your book size. Click on "File" and then "Page Setup". From there go to "Paper Size" and choose your book size. Be sure to click "Apply to Whole Document".

Set your margins to at least .75 on all sides. Click the box that asks if you want "Mirror Margins". Mirror margins will set your manuscript up to be viewed like book pages. While in the "Page Setup" feature, set your gutter to at least 0.1. The gutter is the crease in the middle of the book, where the spine of the book is.

Separate your front matter, body of your manuscript, and your back matter with Section breaks. **This is important when you go to create your headers and footers**. Click on "Page Layout", then "Breaks". Scroll to "Section Breaks." Once there, hit "Section Break, Next Page". You should also use Section Breaks to separate chapters.

Create a header and footer, if desired. Typically, the header of a manuscript will list the title of the book and the author's name. You can put the title on every even page (left) and the author on every odd page (right). Navigate to the "View" feature and click on "Header and Footer". A little box should pop up and your page should go dim, showing the header at the top of the page. Before you type anything, click the boxes that say "Different first page" and "Different odd and even pages." Type directly into the header. You can format the text to the size you want.

Insert page numbers into your footer. Once you pull up the header and footer, you can switch back and forth between them by clicking on the "Switch between header and footer button". Hover the arrow over the buttons located on the toolbar that pops up so that you can see what each button does. Click on the "Insert Page Numbers" to insert your page numbering feature. Again make sure you click the "Different first page" and "Different odd and even pages."

Specify section breaks within your headers and footers. You typically do not want the title and author or page numbers to appear on the front and back matter pages or on the first page of a chapter. This is why you made section breaks. Navigate to the first page of your body text (where you want the title, etc. to appear) and double click on your header (this is just another way to open the header/footer toolbox window). You should have already created Section breaks. Your front matter will be Section 1. Your body text will be Section 2. When in the body text header, click the box on the floating toolbar that says "Same as Previous". **You do not want this header to be "Same as Previous."**

- The header and footers can get tricky depending on the version of Word that you are using. Consult your manual or Help feature for more tips.

- Contact me if you need help with layout. www.karenzomedia.net I can layout your book for your for $50 - $100 (depending on the book size).

Copyright Your Book

So, you have finally finished that novel you started. Or you have put together a book of family recipes or you have written your autobiography. Now you want to insure that no one else can legally use your work for profit. In the United States, there are simple procedures to copyright a written work.

Provide notice of copyright by affixing the copyright symbol to your work. They traditional "c" in a circle or the word "copyright" followed by the date the work was written and your name are sufficient notice of copyright. Technically, your work is copyrighted the moment you set it to paper but you cannot sue for copyright infringement unless you have registered it with the copyright office.

Contact the U.S. Copyright Office to make sure that your work qualifies as a literary work. There are many types of literary works including databases and computer programs. Your work does not have to be published to be copyrighted.

Choose which form to use. You will use the short form only if the work is completely new and you are the sole author. If you used work from other sources, including things you have written, or you have a coauthor then you need the standard TX form.

Include the appropriate payment with your registration. Check the website or call the copyright office to ensure you are enclosing the appropriate amount.

- Generally, copyright remains yours for the length of your life plus 70 years. There are exceptions so check with the copyright office.

- Each country has its own rules on copyright. The United States does have copyright relations with various other countries. Check the website.

Write a Preface

Not every book has to have a preface, but readers do enjoy learning more about how the book you wrote came together. The preface includes a brief description of the book and why you wrote it. It also can contain information on where and how you found your information and also any problems you encountered along the way.

- Write about why you wrote the book. If the book is a work of fiction, then write about how you got the idea for the story.

- Give a brief description of the book. Is it a work of fiction or non-fiction? Give the reader very brief preview of what they will find if they keep turning the pages.

- Tell your readers how you did your research for the book. Did your research involve countless hours at the library, interviews with professionals or a trip to another country? Here is where you briefly relate your research adventures.

- List acknowledgments. Briefly take the time to thank those who helped you along your writing journey. Obviously, you'll never be able to include every single person or institution, so try to keep this is brief as possible without hurting anyone's feelings!

- Recount any troubles you encountered along the way. The journey to write a completed book is strewn with triumphs, failures and near misses. Tell about those adventures in your preface.

Keep it brief. You don't want your preface to stretch more than two pages. Ideally, the preface should be one page or less.

Add Front Matter

Open any book on your shelf and you will find front matter. Front matter consists of the first few pages of your memoir and is a very important element of any professional looking publication. If you plan to distribute your book to family members or you plan to self publish your book, front matter is a must.

- Place your title about one third down and in the center of the first page of your front matter. Put the name of the author here also.

- Put your copyright information, ISBN number and permission to reproduce the content of your memoir on the second page. Also put here any publisher information.

- Make up your dedication to go on the third page. Center this information and place it about half way down the page.

- Use the fourth page to list any acknowledgments you might have. This is the page where you thank all the people who helped you write your memoir.

- Organize your table of contents on the fifth page. Your word processing program can automatically do this for you.

- Place your preface on the sixth page. This page outlines your general purpose for writing your memoir.

- Replace the preface with a forward or prologue, if you wish.

- Don't put page numbers on any of the pages in your front matter.

- Don't use page numbers in your preface. Use lower case roman numerals instead.

Add Back Matter

Before you publish your memoir you need to add back matter to your publication. Back matter is a place for your readers to quickly find various pages in your book. It is also an essential element of all professional publications. Place back matter at the end of your book.

- Put your epilogue on the first page of the back matter. The epilogue consists of any further information you would like to add regarding your memoir. This page is also where you would write about any plans for future volumes. Place your website information in the epilogue.

- Add an appendix. Place in these pages maps, charts and photographs. Label each item in the appendix. For example: Appendix A. Include each of these items in the Table of Contents.

- Make a bibliography. A bibliography is a listing of all the reference materials you used while researching and writing your memoir. Use APA guidelines to format your bibliography. There are programs online that will create the correct format for you.

- Organize an index. This is optional but your readers will appreciate it. You can manually create an Index or your word processor can create one for you.

- Add a photo of yourself. The last page of back matter is often used for biographical information about the writer. Write a brief summary about yourself for this page.

Publishing

Finding Your Publishable Story

So you would like to see your name in print? Many people ask me how to write a publishable memoir. This question always reminds me of Rod Haynes. Rod and I emailed a few times, regarding his book *Rogues Island Memoir*. I can't say that I helped him much, I believe he had completed the book by the time he met me. But I was delighted to speak to someone who had published their memoir.

Rod chose to write about a certain period of his life - his childhood years growing up in the turbulent sixties and living with a sister who would eventually succumb to Cystic Fibrosis.

This is the way to seeing your work published. A published book has a central theme running through it, as in Frank McCourt's *Angela's Ashes*. So your job is to choose a slice of your life to write about.

Ask yourself "What is the one event that shaped my life?"

- Did someone in your family die?
- Did your parents' divorce?
- Have you struggled with an illness?
- Did a best friend come into your life and change the way you looked at the world (think about the movie "My Girl").
- Did a natural disaster or war have an impact on your life?

These are but a few of the challenges you may have faced, I am sure you can think of more.

Make a list of the **core events** in your life. Start with your birth (did something extraordinary happen when you were born?) and then move on through your childhood, young adult years, middle age, etc. You will end up with a list of five to ten items of events. From those events, can you choose one that impacted your life? For Rod there were several events that came together at one period of his life and changed his life forever. And there is the **central theme - life change**. When you have isolated an event, look at it from all angles and write down its key points.

- *How old were you?*

- *What was happening in the world at that time?*
- *What was the value or moral code that existed at that time and how did effect the event?*
- *How did all of these factors come together to create your epiphany?*

Now that you have an event picked out, tell us about it. Don't think about publishing it. Just pretend your children or grandchildren are gathered at your feet and you are going to tell them a story. **Once upon a time I…**

Just tell the story!

Some Thoughts on Publishing

Publishing should never be your main goal when writing *anything*. **Focusing on getting published means that your narrative will never get written.** It brings that inner critic to the foreground and he or she will harass the heck out of you!

When you are finished writing however, you may begin thinking about publishing your memoirs. There are many places to do this. Unless you are famous or have an advanced degree in writing, you can pretty much forget about getting picked up by Random House. 99.9% of the average memoir writers are going to have to self-publish. Very rarely – but it does happen – a book will be so successful that a major house will take notice and pick it up.

Self-Publication

There are many, many places out there offering help with self-publication. You can pay for the printing and these places will list your book on their website and market it for you. In my experience though, the marketing they do is extremely limited. You should be prepared to do the bulk of the marketing on your own. Even traditional publishers expect their authors to do their own marketing!

There are many, many places out there offering help with self-publication. You can pay for the printing and these places will list your book on their website and market it for you. In my experience though, the marketing they do is extremely limited. You should be prepared to do the bulk of the marketing on your own.

Most authors know about offering their books on Amazon. But what are some other venues for selling your books? Some of these are for print books and some are for digital versions of your book. Some of them do both.

Here are some places to sell your book.

Amazon: This is the go-to place for self-publishing these days. Amazon's reach is far and wide and you get the best exposure by publishing with them. They make it easy too! You can create and sell your print version through Create Space and your digital version through KDP (Kindle Direct Publishing). I recommend that you publish the print version through Create Space (www.createspace.com) because once that is done, Create Space sends it right over to KDP for you. You just have to pop over there and fill out the basic info, pricing, etc. and voila! You have a digital copy of your book! When people search for your book on Amazon, they will come to a sales page that shows BOTH versions of the book.

Amazon has a lot of good marketing tools for you too.

Blurb: Blurb is good for print photo books of your vacation or for books that are heavy in photos. Digital books cost you $9.99. You can then sell them on Blurb in your own storefront. Blurb gives you a widget to embed wherever you wish to direct customers to your storefront where they can preview and/or purchase your book.

Book Tango: 100% royalty and markets to major retailers. Watch the <u>introduction video</u>

Kobo Writing Life: Only pays twice per year, so you don't see the profits as often as other venues. Easy to navigate. Your royalty is 70-80%.

Lulu: Books published on Lulu are sold all over the world, through most major bookseller venues. Lulu keeps 10% of the profit, but the wide range of exposure is worth it.

MyEbook: You receive 100% for a short time, then you pay 10% commission to Myebook. Payments are made through PayPal.

Ejunkie: Sell your books in PDF format. This is useful for many businesses and teachers who want to sell a PDF that can be projected on a large screen for a wide audience. Hosting fee of $5 per month with no transaction fees. Upload as many PDFs as you want for just $5 per month.

Nook Press (formerly called PubIt!) This is through Barnes and Noble and reaches a huge portion of readers, especially those who have a Nook. Royalties are 40-60%.

Payhip: Get paid every single time a reader buys your digital book. Payhip takes 5% per transaction. Your profit goes straight to your PayPal account.

Payloadz: Load as many digital books as you want for $14.95 per month. You take away 95% per sale. Pays to PayPal or other bank account.

Smashwords: If your digital book sells on Smashwords site, you keep 80% of the profit. When it sells through one of the major booksellers, your profit is 60%.

A Note on Pricing Your Book

New authors typically set their book prices very high – and sell very little. You want to start out by setting your book at a low price point to increase the numbers of readers you get. It is essential to sales to get the book out there AND reviewed. Think about your own buying habits. Are you going to pay $24.99 for a book with no following and no reviews? Probably not.

Set the price low to start with. My first run of a book is usually set to a price where I receive about $2.00 profit for a sale. Once the reviews start coming in and I have a following, I slowly increase the price.

Think about this. Would you rather sell 10 books at $24.95 and receive about $13 profit ($130) or sell 100 books at $12.99 and receive about $5 profit ($500)? Lower the price!

The Difference between Proofreading and Copy Editing, and between Copy editing and Content Editing

I am frequently asked what the difference is between proofreading and copy editing. Then there is content editing. What is the difference between copy editing and content editing? Contrary to what most authors think, there are distinct differences among the three.

A manuscript should ideally go through each one of these stages in order. Many authors seem to be of the opinion that proofreading is what they need (and all they need). In thinking this, they mistakenly want to pay for proofreading when what they really want is content editing.

Content editing is performed at the rough draft (production) stage of a manuscript. A good content editor will check the manuscript for style, voice, consistency, and overall narrative flow. They will make suggestions as to point of view, character development, audience, plot issues, etc. This is a very in depth analysis of a manuscript. The content editor is trained to spot inconsistencies and other problematic issues with the construction of the narrative.

Copy editing is the next step in the editorial process. The copy editor is responsible for reviewing the grammatical structure of the manuscript, fact checking, and overall consistency of the manuscript (again, in the production stage).

Proofreading is the final stage of the editorial (writing) process. Proofreading is done AFTER the rough draft (production) stage. The manuscript has been reviewed by the content editor for overall narrative flow, and it has been copyedited for serious grammatical issues and correct facts. The proofreader is the final 'eye' of the manuscript. They check for typos, anything the copy editor may have missed, layout of the manuscript (are page numbers correct, are paragraphs indented, are fonts consistent, etc.). The proofreader is NOT the one who will tell you that your character is flat or your plot line is skewed. This is sometimes called **line editing** or **final review**.

Can you get all three from one person? Yes, but it is advisable to have a separate proofreader from the person who did the content and copy editing. Why? Because the proofreader offers a final 'fresh' eye on the manuscript. Having a separate person do the proofreading ensures that issues that the copy editor may have missed are picked up, ensures that the manuscript is laid out correctly, and ensures that pesky typos in the layout stage are caught by 'fresh' eyes.

Do I Need a Proofreader or a Copy Editor?

Online publishing is full of unedited manuscripts. I have even found books formatted for Amazon Kindle, the Nook, etc. published by major houses to be rife with typos. It is a sad thought that our children are reading these manuscripts on their mobile devices and being exposed to improper spelling, grammar, and sentence structure. As an English teacher, I cringe every time I find an error.

I finished writing my book; should I hire a content editor, a copy editor, or a proofreader? Ideally, I would say you need all three. Realistically, at the very least hire a proofreader (the least expensive route). There are some people who advertise themselves as proofreaders, get paid as proofreaders, and perform all three functions. Again, I don't recommend you hire them. Each job is distinct and involved, and someone offering to do all three for very little money is not likely to give you quality. You get what you pay for, right?

I only have enough money to pay for one. Which should I choose? Go with a copy editor. The copy editor is going to clean up your manuscript. Sometimes – if they like you (ha ha just kidding) – they are going to throw in some advice if they see major issues with the content (but don't expect them to rewrite it for you!). THEN, get a family member or friend to read over the final manuscript to catch any glaring typos, etc.

Why is proofreading so important? Your copy editor (or content editor) is going to suggest changes to the manuscript, and you are going to make their changes if you agree with them. In the process of making changes, you risk creating typos and misspellings. Remember, the content and copy editing is done DURING the production of the manuscript. The proofing (line editing, final review) is done AFTER you have made all the changes and the manuscript is ready to go to the printer – **final eyes!**

I have read some beautifully crafted stories on my Kindle – many of them free – but they are not going to make it because NO ONE PROOFREAD THEM! One or two typos is not so bad, but I find it so disheartening to read a great story and get stopped in my reading 'flow' over and over again by grammatical errors and typos. I won't read anything more from that author because it was just so draining to wade through all the messy sentences.

PROOFREAD, I beg you!

Marketing Ideas

❖ Create a website for the book.

❖ Make brochures detailing the highlights of your book and send them out with sales information to places that might be interested – your local museums, libraries, bookstores, restaurants, and schools. I know of one author who wrote about his memories of our small town and sold quite a few copies at the favorite restaurant in town!

❖ Show your book to local bookstores and ask to do a book signing and reading.

❖ Send press releases to your local newspapers announcing your new book. Start local and spread out from there. Tell them you are available for interviews.

❖ Create a blog that contains excerpts of your book.

❖ Contact your local schools and offer to talk to students about your experiences – especially good for war stories.

❖ Don't forget to sell your books to far-flung family members!

❖ Have a family reunion and sell your book there.

❖ Set up a booth at craft fairs and art festivals and offer your book for sale.

❖ Teach a Memoir Writing workshop yourself and sell your book to your students!

GIVE INTERVIEWS about how your product is useful to the average consumer on the radio or for the newspaper. Figure out something about your company that the public would be interested in hearing about. For instance, our accounting firm might pitch an idea for tips on saving money during the recession. Ring up your local radio station and introduce yourself. Be prepared with an idea for a show that they cannot resist.

DEVELOP PODCASTS. These are short videos that air on the Internet and could be as simple as a demonstration of how your product works. Again, find aspects of your business that are marketable at a given time – like the money saving tips in #16.

USE THE INTERNET to its fullest potential. Get your business name all over the World Wide Web. Have a website and offer affiliate packages to people who will list your business on their websites.

BUILD A PROFESSIONAL LOOKING WEBSITE. There are many places where you can build a website relatively cheaply. For a very small monthly fee, you can have your own domain name.

BLOG IT. Start a blog and write short daily blurbs about topics pertaining to your business.

GATHER COMPETITORS' ADS. Keep an eye out for ads and other literature posted around town that pertain to the product you are selling or the service you are offering.

CREATE A WEEKLY OR MONTHLY NEWSLETTER for your clients that highlights issues pertaining to your business and your clients. This newsletter can be an online one or in print or both. Give out copies of the newsletter to new clients and mail copies to existing clients.

SAY IT WITH A PHRASE. Come up with a catchy slogan that potential clients will remember. "If you build it, they will come." The same can be said with "If you say it, they will come." Keep your slogan short and to the point, but make it memorable. Be careful that your slogan is not too cheesy or offensive though or you will be projecting a negative company image.

MAKE AN EBOOK or hire someone to make one for you. A short eBook on issues and subjects of interest to your clients or clients is a great way to get the name of your company out there and highlight your expertise in your area.

How to Promote Your Memoir

You have finished writing your memoir, and you have had it bound and printed. Now it is time to get your baby out into the world. In order to do this, you need to plan a promotion campaign and sell your book. Here are just a few ideas to get you started.

Send the book out into the world. Scour the Internet for other people who have published similar books and send them a copy of your book. Ask for a review and offer to return the favor for them. Be sure to tell them why you think their review would be valuable to you.

Send copies of your book (or an excerpt) to local news editors and request an interview. Many of these editors are always looking for a good filler or local 'celebrities'.

Have a professional website. Most self-publishers (and traditional publishers) provide their authors with a website. You can use the site that they provide you, but I suggest that you have a personal website as well. Doing this will make you look more professional.

Determine who the top distributors are and send a copy of the book to them. These distributors are in the business of finding venues to buy quality books so talk to them about your book. Sell yourself.

Find the local links in your community. If your memoir is about your town, then contact the local historical society and offer to do a reading or donate a copy of your book. If your memoir centers around a health issue, locate the organizations that deal with that particular health issue and offer them a copy of your book.

Get out there! You have to make yourself seen and heard among the multitudes of authors vying for attention.

Leaving and Getting Reviews on Amazon

Reviews can make or break a book (and author) on Amazon. What can authors do to get more reviews? What can readers do when leaving a review? It's only 20 words – help out indie authors by leaving a review!

As one of the leading vendors of online publications, Amazon ratings are extremely important to an Indie (independent) author/publisher. I read books by independent authors more than any other kind of book. Most of my reading is done on my Kindle. I try to always return to Amazon and leave a review for the books that I read. A review doesn't have to be a book report, just 20 short words and you're out of there!

For Readers

Without reviews, a book on Amazon has a slim chance of rising in the ranks. Which means that it has a slim chance of becoming a success. Now there are certainly exceptions. The reviews of *Fifty Shades of Gray* are horrible! 90% of the reviews are negative. Yet, the book skyrocketed to the top of the bestseller's list and the author has a movie deal now. Go figure. The publishing world has always been a crap shoot and still is.

How do readers choose a book? As a reader, think about how you choose a book while shopping on Amazon. Here are my top selling points:

- The cover catches my eye.

- The title sounds interesting.

- The description is short but to the point. (I personally hate long rambling descriptions.)

- The book has more than 10 reviews and most of them are 4's or 5's.

Now, I have purchased books that had no reviews or bad reviews. That was because numbers 1-3 were so strong. I have yet to be disappointed.

So, the reader can't always rely on the reviews to determine whether or not they should read the book.

Fake reviews are unfortunately out there. As a former provider on Elance and Guru, I can tell you that there are way too many authors who are willing to pay professional writers to write reviews for them. I have never and would never do such a thing. I personally would like to expose each and every one of those authors by going to their Amazon site and leaving a negative review. Yeah, it really ticks me off. Anyway, READER BEWARE. Not all is what it seems.

I have also recently heard that some people actually hire people to go in and leave bad reviews. Why? To kill the author's career….revenge for whatever, I suppose. People are sick.

Tips for Reviewers

It will take you less than two minutes, if that. Readers are the lifeblood of any author's career. Your review means life or death to a book published by an Indie author.

Just do it! Amazon requires you to write at least 20 words in your review. That is not much really!

Your rating can make or break an author. Rate the book with 1-5 stars with 5 stars being excellent. This is not a movie rating! This star rating is the MOST important part of your review. Don't give it 3 stars just because you realized you don't like science fiction after all. Don't give it 2 stars because it had a few typos. **IMPORTANT:** Anything under 4 stars can (will) kill the book for the author and greatly damage the author's chance of getting this book anywhere.

Remember what your mama said, "If you can't say something nice, don't say anything at all." Unless the book is absolutely terrible and the author really needs to move into another line of work, please don't rate a book under 4 stars. Indie authors have a hard enough road ahead of them without you taking a stab at them. Just let it go and don't write a review at all.

On another note, if you do find a lot of typos in a book, or you have something to say about the book that you don't want to put in a review, go to the author's page and email them. Indie authors are so much more accessible than traditional authors. And they love to hear from their readers!

___

Tips for Authors/Publishers

Find the book reviewers on Amazon. Look for the top reviewers and offer them a free copy of your book in exchange for a review. Choose reviewers who typically review books that are similar to yours. One post I read suggested targeting 100-300 reviewers. If only a few of those actually respond to you, you will at least get a few reviews for your effort.

Find book reviewers who blog reviews and ask them to review your book on Amazon (and on their blogs).

Read more about asking for book reviews here.
http://www.amazon.com/gp/richpub/syltguides/fullview/RNCWTLEMV71VM

Include comments outside of Amazon. If someone tells you that they like your book or sends you an email telling you how much they liked your book, ask them to post those thoughts on Amazon. Or, if they don't want to take the time to do that, ask them for permission to post their comments on your websites.

Ask family, friends, and colleagues to review your book. Some professionals caution against using reviews from family and friends. A bad review from your second cousin could cause some friction within the family. A glowing review from your mom could appear contrived and hurt your credibility. Ask family and friends to not mention who they are in the review and ask those who don't like the book to just not leave a review at all.

Don't harass anyone after asking once. Not everyone will like your book. Family and friends who don't like the book should feel comfortable about just not leaving a review at all if they didn't care for the book. Hopefully, they will tell you privately! If you are constantly saying, "Why didn't you leave a review?" "Are you going to leave a review?" etc., you are going to make people uncomfortable. Ask once and move on.

Don't respond to negative reviews. It is hard! Resist the temptation, or at the very least, be professional when responding. Twice now I have received sarcastic comments rather than a book review. I answered both of them. The first time I answered back sarcastically. I know I shouldn't have, but I couldn't resist. The second time I just ignored the guy. It wasn't easy.

Report people who don't leave a review but just comment with something totally irrelevant. Unfortunately, there are many people out there who never learned that it is not actually NOT acceptable to say whatever you are thinking. Report them and let it go.

Run contests! a favorite author of mine just ran a contest on his Facebook page. He ran a raffle offering a free signed copy of his next book to 10 people who posted a review on his Amazon title. He then randomly drew 10 names from the reviews. This worked out well for him! And I won the book!

An excellent post about Amazon book reviews: http://annerallen.blogspot.com/2011/11/amazon-reader-reviews-12-things.html

How to Be Your Own Literary Agent

You've written a book you believe is sellable. What now? Should you hire an agent? Agents are not easy to come by if you don't already have a following. It is possible to act as your own agent and sell your book (and other author's) to a publisher. Start with these basic steps and get started being your own literary agent.

Study the business of publishing. You need to be knowledgeable in understanding contracts, royalties, primary and subsidiary rights, copyrights, and other business and legal matters. It is imperative that you know what you are talking about when meeting with publishers.

Know how a book is put together. Knowing what it takes to actually produce a book is important in selling your book to a publisher. It affects how the book is priced, whom it is sold to, and what marketing efforts are needed.

Practice the art of negotiation. Take some books out of your local library and/or sign up for inexpensive classes at your local community college. Also, check with the Small Business Administration for information on workshops and other tips on running a successful business.

Get to know the markets. Check out the bestseller lists, bookstores, and the Writer's Market. Make it part of every business day to do research on potential publishers.

Prepare a killer cover letter and a pitch. A good query letter will have a short paragraph at the beginning that answers the questions: What is this book about? Why should I (the publisher) take it on? What is your angle?

- Be diligent about keeping track of the publishers you submit your work too.

- Always be polite and professional when speaking to a publisher.

- Make sure you pitch your book to the proper editor.

- Never send out simultaneous submissions unless the publisher specifically says that they accept them.

Don't quit. A good agent will uncover every stone and keep submitting.

How to Sell Your Book on the Internet

You've written a book, published it and now you want to sell it. You can go the traditional route of author interviews, book tours and bookstore signings or you can sell your book on the Internet! Internet marketing allows you to reach the small niche markets quickly and easily. Of course, adding some of the above traditional routes won't hurt either. Here are a few tips to selling your book online.

Join the chatter. Sign up with and USE social media. The big ones include

- Facebook
- Linked In
- Twitter
- Goodreads

Build a website. Give your book its own personal home on the World Wide Web. Make the web address the name of the book or your name. I recommend using the actual title of the book so that potential readers can find it faster.

Obtain book reviews. A very important aspect of marketing your book is to find trustworthy people to read and review your book. Research individuals who are experts in the fields you mention in your book and then write to them and ask them for a brief review. The bigger and more important the name of the reviewer the better! Put the reviews on your website.

Visit other author's websites who have published books similar to yours. These authors are often more than willing to write a review for you. You can also use them as a network source by asking them to exchange website links.

Find the small online booksellers. Run a search for small independent booksellers and you will find a huge list of potential sellers willing to virtually 'stock' your book!

Sell your book at the large distributors such as Barnes and Noble, Amazon and Books A Million. Be sure to read the booksellers contract carefully; there are usually fees involved.

Find the places online where writers congregate and start networking. There are many such sites on the Internet and they allow you to post a picture of your book cover, sample pages and contact information.
If you haven't found a publisher for your book yet, consider self-publishing it lulu.com. You can sell the book right at lulu's site.

Keep researching! Selling your book takes time, but with patience the sales will start coming in.

Don't give up!

Press Release Template

Your name   FOR IMMEDIATE RELEASE
Your phone number
Email:

MAIN TITLE OF PRESS RELEASE HERE IN ALL UPPER CASE
Subtitle here in lower case

The lead paragraph includes the who, what, when, where and how of the story

Use enough supporting material to make your case, and to demonstrate that, whatever angle you're promoting, it wasn't something you slapped together carelessly

Finally, spend a sentence or two describing your company and what you do: This paragraph is known as the "boilerplate" Place your boilerplate right above the # # #'s

###

If you would like more information about this topic, or to schedule an interview with {your name}, please call {your name} at {your phone number} or email {your name} at {your email}

Memory Sparkers

Many of these prompts are so personal that you may feel free to destroy your writing when you are finished. Try to allow yourself to write freely about the question, secure in the knowledge that no one ever has to see what you wrote!

Memoir in a Box

Another way to do Memory Sparkers is to cut the paper to individual strips – one memory sparker per strip – then put the strips in a decorative tin, box, or jar. Every day or when the mood strikes you, pull out one strip in write about it. *(You can purchase Memoir in a Box or Journal in a Jar from www.double-roads.com).*

- ❑ Tell about the worst fight/argument you ever had

- ❑ Where did you spend your honeymoon?

- ❑ Write about a gift you once received that had special meaning for you.

- ❑ Write a bit about your favorite toy as a child.

- ❑ What was your favorite book as a child? Why?

- ❑ What is your favorite book as of today? Why?

- ❑ Write about an event that still hurts to remember.

- ❑ How did you choose your profession or career?

- ❑ What are you afraid to have others know about you?

- ❑ If you could change one thing about your life, what would it be?

- ❑ What is the one thing you regret most in your life?

- ❑ Talk about some things in this world that annoy you.

- ❑ What is the hardest thing you have ever had to do?

- ❑ What was your most memorable holiday experience?

- ❑ When and how did you learn the truth about Santa Claus?

- ❑ Did you ever build a playhouse, fort, or treehouse?

- ❑ Did you ever lose something that was valuable to you?

- Were you ever locked out (or in) of someplace?

- When and how did you ever outsmart someone?

- Did you ever perform in front of an audience?

- Did you ever stick up for a friend?

- Did you ever get lost?

- Did you ever run away from home?

- Write about the best concert you ever attended

- Draw a picture or describe in words (or both!) your childhood home.

- Write about a gift you once received that had special meaning for you.

- What was your most memorable holiday experience?

- What questions would you like to have answered?

- Where do you go when you feel you need to 'get away from it all'?

- If a movie were made of your life, what star would play you? Why?

- What is the one thing in the world that couldn't be paid to do?

- What are some of things you do when you're depressed?

- What is the most bizarre thing you have ever seen?

- What is the most important lesson you would like to share with future generations?

- What event in history has always intrigued you?

- Tell about your most joyful life experience.

- Write about some of the things your parents used to say

- Talk about what you wanted in a partner as a young man/woman. Then talk about how your expectations changed as you grew older.

- What is your deepest, darkest secret?

- If you could change one thing about your life, what would it be?

- Talk about your saddest life experience.

- What do you think the meaning of life is?

- List some things that you are disappointed about.

- What are some things that you find hard to share with others?

- Write an unsent letter to someone who has annoyed you or you are still angry at.

- What is the one thing you regret most in your life?

- Talk about some things in this world that annoy you.

- What is the hardest thing you have ever had to do?

- What makes you sad?

- Where do you stand spiritually? Do you believe in God? Talk about the feelings you have toward spirituality.

- What are some rules that you have broken?

- What are you afraid to have others know about you?

- Finish the sentence, "I've never told anyone that…"

- At what age die you feel you had finally grown up?

- Write about an event that still hurts to remember.

LINKS

JOURNALING WEBSITES

KARENZO MEDIA & LIFETALES. Preserving History and Healing Lives…One Lifestory at a Time. www.karenzomedia.net

INSPIRED TO JOURNAL: includes articles on journaling, exercises, quotes, and prompts. http://www.inspiredtojournal.com/

THE CENTER FOR JOURNAL THERAPY: A gathering place for those who know the power of writing for growth and healing. http://www.journaltherapy.com/

Porter, Kay. **LIVE YOUR CREATIVE VISION**. http://www.kporterfield.com/memoir/Memoir_Index.html Good ideas and prompts.

MEMOIR WRITING WEBSITES

KARENZO MEDIA & LIFETALES Preserving History and Healing Lives…One Lifestory at a Time. www.karenzomedia.net

CAPTURING MEMORIES: STARTING A MEMOIR WRITING GROUP IS EASY http://www.capturingmemories.com/home.html

Porter, Kay. **LIVE YOUR CREATIVE VISION**. http://www.kporterfield.com/memoir/Memoir_Index.html Good ideas and prompts.

Lincoln, Eleanor, CSJ. SELF-**KNOWLEDGE THROUGH WRITING YOUR MEMOIR**. http://www.goodgroundpress.com/index.asp?PageAction=VIEWCATS&Category=14 A retired professor of English from The College of St. Catherine, Dr. Lincoln has given numerous workshops on memoir writing.

Books and Articles on Autobiography

Olney, James. *Metaphors of Self: The Meaning of Autobiography*. Princeton: Princeton University Press, 1972

Starobinski, Jean, "The Style of Autobiography," *Autobiography: Essays Theoretical and Critical*. ed. James Olney. Princeton, New Jersey: Princeton University Press, 1980. p. 74

White, Michael and David Epston. *Narrative Means to Therapeutic Ends*. WW Norton & Company: New York. 1990

Malinowski, Bronislaw. "The Role of Myth in Life". *Sacred Narrative*. Dundes, Alan, ed., Los Angeles: University of California Press, 1984.

Harjo, Joy. *The Spiral of Memory Interviews*. Coltelli, Laura, Editor. University of Michigan Press. 1996

Muske, Carol. Women and Poetry: Truth, Autobiography, and the Shape of Self. University of Michigan Press. 1997

Baldwin, Christina. *Life's Companion: Journal Writing as a Spiritual Quest*. New York: Simon and Schuster, 1990.

Conway, Jill Ker. When Memory Speaks. New York: 1998).

Gilmour, Peter. *The Wisdom of Memoir: Reading and Writing Sacred Texts*. Winona, MN: Saint Mary's Press, 1997.

Goldberg, Natalie. *Writing Down the Bones: Freeing the Writer Within*. Boston: Shambhala, 1986.

Goldberg, Natalie. *Wild Mind: Living the Writer's Life*. New York: Bantam, 1990.

Inventing the Truth: The Art and Craft of Memoir. Ed. William Zinsser. Boston: Houghton Mifflin, 1987.

Moffat, Mary Jane. *The Times of Our Lives: A Guide to Writing Autobiography and Memoir*. Santa Barbara: John Daniel, 1989.

Welty, Eudora. *One Writer's Beginning*. New York: Warner, 1984.

Recommended Memoirs

Tales of the Brooklyn Hobo by Alexander Procho

Angela's Ashes by Frank McCourt

Tis by Frank McCourt

All Souls: A Family Story from Southie by Michael Patrick MacDonald

The Nazi's Officers Wife by Edith Hahn Beer

Dry by Augusten Burrows

Running with Scissors by Augusten Burrows

A Million Little Pieces by James Frey

My Friend Leonard by James Frey

The Autobiography of My Mother by Jamaica Kincaid

The Woman Warrior by Maxine Hong Kingston

Their Eyes Were Watching God by Zora Neale Hurston

Stolen Lives: Twenty Years in a Desert Jail by Malika Oufkir

The Bell Jar by Sylvia Plath

I Know Why the Caged Bird Sings by Maya Angelou

Diary of a Young Girl by Anne Frank

Falling Leaves: The Memoir of an Unwanted Chinese Daughter by Adeline Yen Mah

Coming of Age in Mississippi by Anne Moody

Lost in Place: Growing Up Absurd in Suburbia by Mark Salzman

My Brother by Jamaica Kincaid

Memories of a Catholic Girlhood by Mary McCarthy

Bad Boy: A Memoir by Walter Dean Myers

Without a Map: A Memoir by Meredith Hall

This Boy's Life: A Memoir by Tobias Wolff

Teacher Man: A Memoir by Frank McCourt

The Tender Bar: A Memoir by by J. R. Moehringer

Dog Years: A Memoir by Mark Doty

The Birthday Party: A Memoir of Survival by Stanley Alpert

Waking: A Memoir of Trauma and Transcendence by Matthew Sanford

Chosen by a Horse: A Memoir by Susan Richards

My Father's Secret War: A Memoir by Lucinda Franks

What Remains: A Memoir of Fate, Friendship, and Love by Carole Radziwill

Stealing Buddha's Dinner: A Memoir by Bich Minh Nguyen

Magical Thinking: True Stories by Augusten Burroughs

God Grew Tired of Us: A Memoir by John Bul Bul Dau, Michael Sweeney, Michael S. Sweeney

Funny in Farsi: A Memoir of Growing up Iranian in America by Firoozeh Dumas

Easter Everywhere: A Memoir by Darcey Steinke

Unwanted: A Memoir by Kien Nguyen

Persian Girls: A Memoir by Nahid Rachlin

Long Way Gone: Memoirs of a Boy Soldier by Ishmael Beah

Rewind, Replay, Repeat: A Memoir of Obsessive-Compulsive Disorder by Jeff Bell

Leaving Church: A Memoir of Faith by Barbara Brown Taylor

Infidel by Ayaan Hirsi Ali

Unbowed: A Memoir by Wangari Maathai

The Color of Water: A Black Man's Tribute to His White Mother by James McBride

Seamstress: A Memoir of Survival by Sara Tuvel Bernstein, Louise Toots Thornton, Marlene Bernstein Samuels

Out of Egypt: A Memoir by Andre Aciman

Bookbinding/Printing

GIGA BOOKS. Quick and easy bookbinding for writers and others who want to see their words in print. Learn to make your own trade paperbacks and hardcover books. http://www.gigabooks.net/

CLICK BOOK. A powerful yet easy-to-use printing utility, lets you print customized day planner pages, wallet booklets, church bulletins, brochures, greeting cards, posters, business cards, flipbooks, catalogs, banners, microfiche, CD covers and more from Internet, Windows, or CD-Rom files! ClickBook, helps you scale and rotate digital photos, e-mails, documents, favorite on-line content, or other critical information into 170+ mobile and convenient layouts. You can even design your own custom layouts and save up to 75% in paper costs! http://www.bluesquirrel.com/products/clickbook/

BOOK ASSEMBLY PHOTO-JOURNAL. Make your own books. a photo journal that walks you through the process of book binding. http://tobycraig.livejournal.com/29223.html

DO IT YOURSELF BOOK PRESS. Lots of useful information on book binding techniques. Helpful whether or not you are planning to bind your own books. http://nomediakings.org/doityourself/doityourself_book_press.html

LULU. Tools and services to make publishing simple and the most options to sell your books. Create print books, ebooks, photo books, audiobooks, and more. This is a print on demand site that also offers a marketplace to sell your books. This book that you are reading was printed through Lulu. http://www.lulu.com.

WORDCLAY. FREE DIY self-publishing wizard, they also offer a variety of services to help you create, distribute and promote a marketable book. http://www.wordclay.com

Publishing Links

BAR CODE: Bookland EAN/13 with add on.

ISBN: R. R. Bowker for block of 10 numbers. The charge is $225 per block. www.bowkerlink.com

LIBRARY OF CONGRESS CATALOG CARD NUMBER: Preassigned card Numbers (PCN) appear on the copyright page of each book and are also included in the lists and reviews appearing in the leading journals of the book trade. LC numbers are essential if selling to libraries. LC number must be requested prior to publication.

DUOTROPE'S DIGEST (Novel, short fiction, and poetry market database and a Query tracker.) www.duotrope.com/index

QUERYTRACKER DATABASE (Lists thousands of agents) www.querytracker.net/qlist.php

PUBLISHERS MARKETPLACE (Check out publishers and learn more about publishing basics)

WRITER'S MARKET www.writersmarket.com

WRITING EFFECTIVE PRESS RELEASES
http://www.marketingsource.com/pressrelease/writingrelease.html

297+ MARKETING IDEAS. http://www.goodmarketingideas.com/

WRITER'S PLANNER: AN ONLINE WRITER'S TRACKING TOOL
http://writersplanner.com/

WORDPRESS (free blogging) www.wordpress.com

PAY PAL www.paypal.com

LEADING A LIFETALES WORKSHOP: A GUIDE TO BOOKING AND LEADING WORKSHOPS ON LIFEWRITING www.lulu.com/content/1159376

Organizations for Writers

NATIONAL ASSOCIATION OF WOMEN WRITERS. "As women writers we seek to - encourage... teach... inspire... motivate... entertain... NAWW is Where Women Unite To Write."

NATIONAL WRITERS ASSOCIATION. The NWA "provides education and an ethical resource for writers at all levels of experience." This organization sponsors annual contests, offers contract reviews, manuscript critiques, research findings relevant to writers, editing services, a professional freelancers directory and more to members.

THE NATIONAL WRITERS UNION. "The National Writers Union is more than just another writers association - it is the only labor union that represents freelance writers in all genres, formats, and media".

POETRY SOCIETY OF AMERICA. The oldest poetry writers association in the US, offering support for all poets from professionals to unpublished writers.

AUSTRALIAN SOCIETY OF AUTHORS. The ASA was developed "to promote and protect the rights of Australia's authors and illustrators". This writers association provides a contract advisory service, runs mentorships for new and emerging writers and offers advice about writing, copyright and publishing.

FELLOWSHIP OF AUSTRALIAN WRITERS. The "FAW is active on behalf of writers in areas such as government policy, literary awards, professional advice, representation of writers' rights and the promotion of literature".

SMALL PUBLISHERS, ARTISTS & WRITERS NETWORK (SPAWN)
PMB 123
323 E. Matilija St., Suite 110
Ojai, CA 93023
Telephone 818-886-4281
Fax: 818-886-3320
SPAWN membership dues are $45 per year.

FLORIDA PUBLISHERS ASSOCIATION, INC.
P.O. Box 430
Highland City, FL 33846-0430
Phone: 863-647-5951
Fax: 863-647-5951
FPAbooks @ aol.com
www.FLbookpub.org
Dinah Arnette, President
Betsy Lampe, Association Executive

Publishers, self-publishers, authors and vendors: send this completed form (Member Application) with your check, money order, or PayPal payment ($100 for publishers/$150 for vendors) to:

SPAN, SMALL PUBLISHERS ASSOCIATION OF NORTH AMERICA
http://www.SPANnet.org
SPAN is a dynamic organization for small publishers. Run by publishing consultants, Tom and Marilyn Ross, SPAN membership includes important money-saving possibilities, an outstanding monthly newsletter, and an optional yearly publishing seminar. $105, $70 if member of FLPA

PUBLISHER'S MARKETING ASSOCIATION PMA ONLINE
http://pma-online.org
Publisher's Marketing Association, one of the best organizations for publishers. Offers all SPAWN members a discount on PMA memberships. Instead of their usual fee of $99, SPAWN members may join PMA for only $73. Offers all SPAWN members a $35 discount on SPAN memberships.

NATIONAL ASSOCIATION OF WOMEN WRITERS (NAWW). Offers all SPAWN members a $10 discount on NAWW memberships.

ASSOCIATION OF AUTHORS AND PUBLISHERS (AAP).
6124 Hwy. 6 North, PMB #109
Houston, TX 77084
Phone: 281-340-0185
cathy @ idealady.com
www.authorsandpublishers.org
Cathy Stucker, President

PUBLISHERS ASSOCIATION OF THE SOUTH
4124 Indigo Pl.
Florence, SC 29501
Phone: 843-662-2800
Fax: 843-662-2550
executive @ pubsouth.org
www.pubsouth.org
President: Beth Wright
Gina Evans, Association Executive

About the Author

Karen Silvestri is co-owner of Karenzo Media and an instructor of English Composition and Reading at Fayetteville Technical Community College and Robeson Community College. She currently teaches part-time and is the Instructional Specialist for the Learning Center at Robeson Community College in Lumberton, N.C. She is the author of several non-fiction books geared towards education. She enjoys art journaling and teaching memoir workshops.

karenzomedia@gmail.com

Karenzo Media www.karenzomedia.net
Hamilton Academy http://hamiltonacademy.net/
My Altered Art http://nonnakaren.wordpress.com/

Former Clients include Craig Valentine, Impack Fitness, Talking Memories, Fresh Word Ministries, First Pentecostal Holiness, Real Kids Photography, Demand Studios, Florida Living Magazine, Random Order Entertainment, The Jupiter Farmer, The Stuart News, Women Service Network, The Street Called Straight Tabernacle, Photographs by Nancy, Adventure Horizons Magazine, numerous fiction authors, Florida Georgia Blood Alliance, City of Port St. Lucie Parks & Recreation, Suite 101, Bella Online, St. Gerard Campus, The Life Center, Literary Mama.

Feedback from Clients

"I love the ebook this provider prepared! She went over and above the scope of the project with very little direction. Great writing, design and layout. I highly recommend Karen for all of your writing needs."

"This was a rush job and the writer was able to deliver on time and within my cost parameters. Would absolutely work with this writer again!"

"Great job ... would contract with provider again!"

"Thank you so much for the excellent work you did on this e-book. You turned it around quicker than I expected and with the highest level of quality. I will definitely be contacting you again in the upcoming months. Thanks so much!" – Craig Valentine

"Karen was FANTASTIC and delivers high quality work!I like very much what you've done here, Karen. You're good at what you do. Thank you." – Compare Las Vegas Weddings

"I am very happy with what you have done. Thank you very much for your fast and excellent work. Look forward to working with you further in the future, when I have other work of this nature to do." – The Happy Well Fed Artist

"Karen was very insightful in addition to being a talented, intelligent writer. She brought the direction and encouragement I needed to knock this proposal out of the park. You will not regret hiring her for your project!" – Mills Creative Mind

"Extremely satisfied! The eBook project was a complex one, because while coming up with interesting benefits to offer its readers, the subject matter also had to fit the related website and its marketing goals. Karen (of Karenzo Media) did a spectacular job. Her creativity, professionalism, and dedication to the project were all first-rate. We are extremely satisfied with the quality, delivery, and pricing of the product. It was a great pleasure working with Karen, and I look forward to doing further projects together in the near future. I would absolutely recommend her to anyone. You will not regret it!' – Talking Memoires

"I am very pleased with the final product. I got more than I expected quality, delivery, price and service. I would definitely work with Karen again." -Coffee 2 Tea

"Karen followed the outline to a T and provided the product I was needing. She is on my list of providers for use on future products."

"Exactly what I needed. Excellent work done as instructed and provided on time. A rare feat. Highly recommend." – Joe Kaiser, Real Estate Investor

"Quick and professional. Enjoyed working with Karen!"

"We required some rewrite and rework of the photographs in the report, and they were done cheerfully and quickly. Very professional and nice to work with." -Real Kids Photography

More Books by Karenzo Media

Creative Writing Workshop for Middle & High School Students by Karen Hamilton Silvestri

A hit with English and Creative Writing teachers! Over 165 pages of exercises for your English and Creative Writing class! How to write in different genres (sci-fi, fantasy, newspaper, children's books, plays, poetry and more!) Also includes important grammar issues such as sentence fragments and run-on sentences. Plan a semester or a full year around these lessons. The Kindle edition is formatted so that you can quickly find a writing lesson when you need it. How many times have you had 10 minutes to fill in class and were at a loss how to fill the time? Pull out your Kindle and get a quick idea for a fun writing assignment for your students. Includes individual and group work. Perfect for Homeschoolers! (pdf and Kindle)

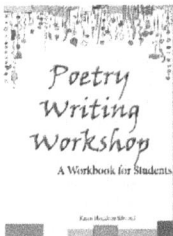

Poetry Writing Workshop: A Workbook for Students by Karen Hamilton Silvestri

This book describes easy to follow directions for creating poems that touch the heart. It includes writing exercises and prompts for traditional poems like the cinquain and haiku and more modern poetry like generated poems and found poetry. No matter what age you are, these exercises will show you how easy it is to jump into writing poetry! Written by English and Creative writing teachers for their students from middle school to adult. (pdf and Kindle)

Playing with Words: A Poetry Workshop by Karen Hamilton Silvestri

What is better than reading and writing poetry? Creating poems! This workbook is for older students and adults who want to play with words. There are 12 ideas (exercises) for creating poems by playing with words here, as well as a few examples of poems created by myself and famous poets like Lewis Carroll. The print version has space for students to write in. The Kindle version has those pages removed. (pdf and Kindle)

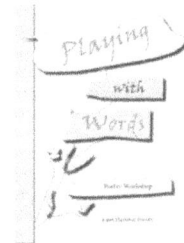

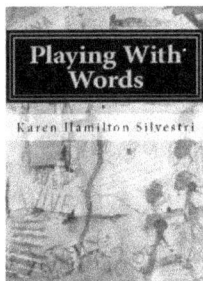

Playing with Words by Karen Hamilton Silvestri

This workbook includes exercises for the younger crowd (middle school age) and for older students and adults who want to play with words. There are 30 exercises for creating poems by playing with words here, as well as a few examples of poems created by myself and famous poets like Lewis Carroll, Robert Frost, Shakespeare, Dylan Thomas, and Elizabeth Bishop. Play with writing cut-ups, sonnets, villanelles, found poetry, permutations, and more!

Teachers (and others) are loving these exercises! Find this book on Amazon.com

Short Story Writing Workshop: A Workbook for Students by Karen Hamilton Silvestri

Looking for writing exercises for students? In this workbook you will find 10 focused exercises that build a student's confidence towards writing their very own short story. The short story workbook walks the student through 10 exercises that focus on plot, setting, dialogue, conflict, and more! The workbook includes exercises in helping students come up with an idea for a short story and mapping out their story. (pdf and Kindle)

Fiction Writing Workbook

Exercises for Teens in Writing General Fiction, Science Fiction, Fantasy, Plays, and Children's Books

Karen Hamilton Silvestri

Fiction Writing Workshop for Teens: Review and Practice **Worksheets for Middle and High School Students** by Karen Hamilton Silvestri
A hit with English and Creative Writing teachers! Over 75 pages of exercises for your English and Creative Writing class! This workbook contains instructions and individual exercises for writing general fiction, science fiction, fantasy, children's books, and plays. Plan a semester or a full year around these lessons. Exercises are on individual pages so that you can quickly find a writing lesson when you need it. How many times have you had 10 minutes to fill in class and were at a loss how to fill the time? Pull out this workbook and get a quick idea for a fun writing assignment for your students. Includes individual and group work. Give a workbook to each student in your Creative Writing class! No more photocopying! Perfect for Homeschoolers! Find this book on Amazon.com

Writing Your Memoirs Workshop: A Manual for Instructors by Karen Hamilton Silvestri
Updated and expanded in 2012, the manual for instructors has more than ever resources to help lead memoir writing workshops in your community! Includes many tools for a potential instructor – how to find venues, how to advertise, what to charge, how to run the workshop, what to do after the workshop, and so much more! It includes sample handouts and sample promotional materials. A helpful guide to help you get started leading workshops on memoir writing in your community. I have been leading workshops since 1998 and share with you my ideas, my research. (pdf and Kindle)

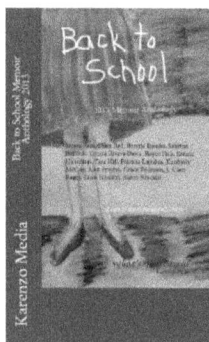

Back to School Memoir Anthology 2013 September 22, 2013 978-1492775218
If there is one memory we can't bury, it is most likely a school memory. Whether you attended public or private school, or you were taught at home, you spent some time of your life learning. Many of us tend to gravitate towards the bad memories of school, and I am sure that everyone has at least one bad memory or embarrassing moment, but I was relieved and happy to see that many choose to focus on the successes and the joy of school as well. This compilation of memoirs encompasses the good and the not so good memories of being in school. I would like to thank all of the people who contributed to this anthology . The authors here are teachers, artists, authors, and professionals from all walks of life. (Print, pdf, or Kindle)

What's Your Story Memoir Anthology 2013 978-0989931847
This anthology brings together the work of a group of special people who had the courage to not only write down their memories, but to share them with the world. We are pleased to bring you this collection of stories telling about special people, trials and triumphs, firsts and favorites, and overcoming adversities. We hope you enjoy these stories and are encouraged to write down your own life stories. Enter your story in the What's Your Story Memoir Anthology 2014! (Print, pdf, or Kindle)

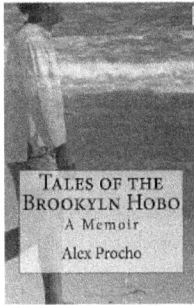

Tales of the Brookyln Hobo: A Memoir by Alex Procho 978-0-9798164-7-5

Tales of the Brooklyn Hobo is a haunting and engaging tale of the adventures of a Brooklyn man who sets out to explore the country and finds heartache, wonder, and a new sense of self in the Age of Aquarius. This memoir chronicles Alex's adventures as he hops a freight train in Nebraska, is harassed by the federales in Mexico, has a gun pulled on him by a tearful Oregonian cowboy, encounters God while tripping on LSD at Woodstock, and finds love in all the wrong places. Intermixed in the narrative of the past are journal entries (called Night Flights), which address the author's struggle with Bipolar Disorder and drug addiction. A native of Brooklyn, NY, Alex has traveled the country extensively in his quest for truth and identity. He has battled addictions - his own and the people around him - for as far back as he can recall. Diagnosed with Bipolar Disorder, Alex reveals with candor and humor how the disorder has affected his life. He also gives his audience a glimpse into his battle to come to terms with his addiction to pain pills and alcohol. (Print, pdf, or Kindle)

The Caver King by Enzo Silvestri 978-0-9798164-6-8

THE CAVER KING tells the story of Tsami, a brash youth in search of adventure, and Tsado, a sedentary book-wise scholar. Tsami's dreams of swashbuckling adventure are realized one day when he and Tsado are visited by the "King's Commissioner', who assigns them to a task in service of the High King's Army. After accepting the Commission, they find that there are many obstacles to overcome, and many discoveries to be made. During the journey, they find out that they are not alone in their quest. (Print or Kindle)

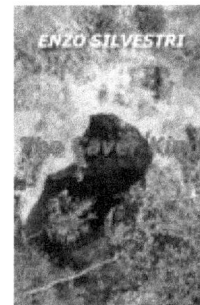

Rock of Ages by Enzo Silvestri 978-0-9798164-9-9

The Rock of Ages introduces a world that is headed towards a one world government. The Book of Revelation comes to life in this fast-paced, historically accurate novel. A dramatization of the New Testament Book of Revelation, the *Thief in the Night* trilogy departs from the much loved *Left Behind* series in that the characters 'stay behind' willingly. The story is set chiefly in Australia and Israel and tells the story of four friends and their involvement in developments at the end of the age. (Print or Kindle)

Thief in the Night by Enzo Silvestri 978-0-9798164-5-1

In the second book of the *Thief in the Night* trilogy, we follow the Aussies on an international whirlwind that reunites them explosively in Israel, and not just from the weapons. Effie's fiancée is executed on the drug-ridden streets of Sydney, she holds god personally responsible, and cynically withdraws from her devout Christian life, turning her energies to teaching. Her colleague Rafi's words seem laughable when he suggests to his Israeli friend Erez, a Lebanon war veteran, that Effie would be a good catch. Neroux, with the 'Gift of the Gab' rises to the dizzy heights of President of the Union seemingly overnight. Were his DEFT and CP a breath of fresh air to the dying, starving world, or are there other more sinister motivations to his schemes? (Print or Kindle)

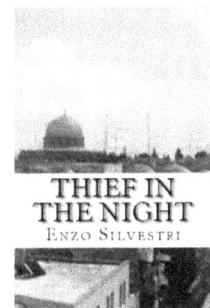

The Fig Tree by Enzo Silvestri. 978-0-9899318-3-0

The final book in the trilogy is a story of beginnings. Rafi had only started driving cabs as a stop-gap measure in between jobs. Effie and Ben had a great life to look forward to. They would surely get married, and have many children, while living the ideal life, or so it seemed. Erez too needed a change of scenery, and not just to the beaches of Eilat. He survived the war, but the loss of his school friends, weighed heavily upon him. His uncle's advice had him jetting halfway around the world to find his destiny in a rocky desert landscape, and in unexpected circumstances that would entwine all of their destinies. (Print or Kindle)

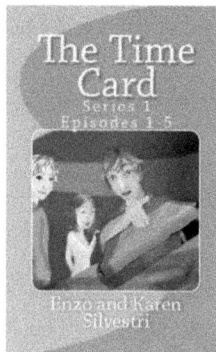

The Time Card series follows the adventures and fortunes of three friends – Blue, Jesse, and Ellie – as they use the contents of their newly found case to travel to diverse and exotic places. Their middle school studies come alive as they interact with historical figures of their country and the world, while at the same time struggling to not change the time-line or upset the course of history. Trying to hide the case from present day bullies, the friends try to stay one step ahead of their arch enemies Ryan Johnson and Jake Barker, not to mention sinister otherworld forces who are determined to find the time card. Join the kids as they explore new worlds, battle bullies, deal with family issues, and ultimately try to save the world. The Time Card is aimed at young readers as short stories that can be read in a single sitting. The Time Card series. Anyone will enjoy the stories while learning about history, dealing with social situations, and improving vocabulary and reading skills.

The Time Card Series, Episodes 1-5 (Print or Kindle)

The Time Card Series, Episode 1 *The Mysterious Case*: **Short Reads for Middle School**
Written by Enzo Silvestri with Karen Hamilton Silvestri, Illustrations by Megan McMillan
978-1481294331
Now includes a study guide and writing prompts!
In the first book of the series Blue, Jesse, and Ellie find something strange while fishing. Nothing ever happens in St Andrews, a sleepy little town in North Carolina. Nothing that is, until the appearance of a small tightly sealed metal case. The three middle school friends, 13 year-olds Australian-born Blue, his neighbor Jesse, and Jesse's sister Ellie live in these backwoods. One day they stumble upon the metal case in a creek while they are fishing. What's inside it? How can they open it since it has no catches or hinges? There's something in it, as they can feel the contents rolling around inside. The three friends lose badly as they resist bullies on the bus, but can they turn it all around by using their new time card?

The Time Card Series, Episode 2 *Declaration Time*: **Short Reads for Middle School**
Written by Enzo Silvestri with Karen Hamilton Silvestri, Illustrations by Megan McMillan 978-1481296304
In this episode the pilot of the craft that jettisoned the mysterious case meets with a mysterious Admiral and is tasked with retrieving the case before evil forces find it. On earth, Blue, Jesse, and Ellie accidently find themselves in 1776. After Jesse accidently changes the course of history, the friends must race to save Thomas Jefferson before the power runs out on their chronometer. (Print or Kindle)

The Time Card Series, Episode 3 *Rebooted*: **Short Reads for Middle School** Written by Enzo Silvestri with Karen Hamilton Silvestri, Illustrations by Megan McMillan 978-1481298681
In episode 3, the pilot who jettisoned the Time Card case, Tam Harnik, heads for earth and encounters trouble with tracking the time card. Blue, Jesse, and Ellie must deal with the nosy Ryan and Jake, who have been snooping around the computer shed. The three friends find themselves chasing the bullies through the past, trying to stop them from upsetting history and changing all their histories. Will they save the timeline? Or will a change in the timeline be something they find they actually want to keep? (Print or Kindle)

The Time Card Series, Episode 4 *Escape from Harvard*: **Short Reads for Middle School**
Written by Enzo Silvestri with Karen Hamilton Silvestri, Illustrations by Megan McMillan 978-1481299251
In episode 4, Tam Harnik, the pilot from afar continues his search for the missing Time Card case. He tries to remain undetected in the small town of St. Andrews by melting in with the general population. Ellie has a school paper due and talks Blue and Jesse into using the time card to gather research at Harvard. The kids run into trouble when Harvard security questions why three kids are on campus and Ellie tells them the truth. Blue and Jesse have to rescue her from the flabbergasted adults. (Print or Kindle)

The Time Card Series, Episode 5 *Civil Rivalry*: **Short Reads for Middle School** Written by Enzo Silvestri with Karen Hamilton Silvestri, Illustrations by Megan McMillan 978-1490362625
In the final episode of the first series, Jake Barker and Ryan Johnson steal the time card, and the three friends must hurry to find it (and Barker) before history is changed. The Daktars threaten again, and Commander Tam Harnik hones in on the kids and the time card. (Print or Kindle)

The Time Card Series, Episode 6 *War in the Heavens*: **Short Reads for Middle School** Written by Enzo Silvestri with Karen Hamilton Silvestri, Illustrations by Megan McMillan 978-0-9899318-1-6
In Episode 6 of the Time Card Series, the three friends find themselves in a Daktar jail cell after being abducted by the Daktar alien rebels. Tam and his fighters rush to rescue the kids and find themselves in the fight of their lives. Meanwhile, Blue, Jesse, and Ellie won't sit by and wait to be rescued; they take matters into their own hands. (Print or Kindle)

www.ingramcontent.com/pod-product-compliance
Lightning Source LLC
LaVergne TN
LVHW061248060426

835508LV00018B/1546